Travellers' T

from the Bord....

Fred Kennington

Dedicated to Gordon Wilson without whose memories this book would never have been started and whose friendship over many years has been so much valued.

Acknowledgments to all those who have contributed by relating their memories and by making photographs available. They are too numerous to list individually. Every effort has been made to avoid infringing copyright. The author apologises should there have been any unintended omission.

Published by F L Kennington, Northumbria House, 35 Corbar Road, Stockport, Cheshire, SK2 6EP.

Designed and produced for the publisher from computerised origination by John Banks, Romiley, Cheshire. British Library Cataloguing-in-Publication Data - a catalogue record for this book is available from the British Library. Printed in Wales by WBC Book Manufacturers, Bridgend, Mid-Glamorgan.

CONTENTS

1. FOREWORD

Remembering buses? Why? They aren't very interesting. Maybe not, but they were part of our social history in years gone by. At the end of the 20th century there are signs that they may even be making a comeback.

As a little laddie I was always interested in cars and buses. We had weekly tickets between Berwick and Spittal to keep me amused.

I went to work, first on the railway, and from 1949, on the buses, spending all my working life in the industry.

It was more labour intensive then as most buses had conductors. All sorts of incidents occurred, occasionally serious, many funny, but always 'different'. Having started to make Oral History recordings for Berwick Record Office as a 'Friend' of that Archive, I recorded the memories of some bus staff and talked with others. Just how much history had been lost, and how much more would soon be lost, if not written down, launched me into writing this book.

I'm not setting out to record intimate technical details of the buses. I want to remember the people who used them and who worked on them - and their history - for the Borough of Berwick-upon-Tweed.

2. WHERE IS BERWICK UPON TWEED?

It stands on the Northumberland coast at the most northerly point in England, roughly midway between Newcastle and Edinburgh at sixty miles from each.

If you don't know much about the place, do read a bit about its history. It is unique in having changed hands between England and Scotland fourteen times before eventually becoming English. It has the remnants of Edwardian walls dating from 1300 and wonderfully preserved Elizabethan walls.

Local government reorganisation in 1974 saw the Borough boundary extended south to include Glendale and Seahouses thus covering a large area but with only 29,000 inhabitants.

Berwick, itself, is the focal point for part of south east Scotland so something about the buses and bus people in that area has been included.

3. A CHANGING COMMODITY

If you want to get about you need transport. Private cars were not always within the means of many so buses were part of everyday life - indeed not that many years ago they were vital to most of the population.

Transport is a changing thing - packhorses, stagecoaches, canals, railways, trams, buses; one has superseded the other. With road traffic ever increasing it seems we may see the clock being turned back. Manchester brought trams back on to its city streets not long ago, its Metrolink. Far from being the archaic form of transport killed off fifty years ago, it is the most favoured form in the city.

Back in history Berwick was an important seaport. The easiest way to travel distances - if you could afford to do so - was by ship, with regular services to the Tyne, to London, and to Leith.

For the bulk of the population it was either walk or use the local carriers. Using horse-drawn wagons with tarpaulin covers, their function was to carry goods and produce between market towns and villages. They ran on regular days, once or twice a week, and would take the odd passenger at a low fare provided that the passenger could accept a slow journey while deliveries were made.

In due course rough tracks were replaced by rather better roads allowing stage coaches to come into use after about 1760. They were expensive both to provide and to use and were within the means of only the rich.

With the advent of railways, which came to Berwick in 1846, stagecoaches became redundant but carriers, whose work was localised, continued to serve the country areas until the early 20th century.

As motor vehicles were developed, a process hastened by the 1914-18 War, they began to provide transport for all. Buses came into their own and railways went into decline.

By 1960 private transport had come into fashion and bus services went into decline. Forty years later the surfeit of private cars is seen as unsustainable.

Wagonette, circa 1910. Probably a party from Spittal. *(Berwick Record Office)*

THE
Royal William
COACH,
BETWEEN
NEWCASTLE AND BERWICK.

The Public are respectfully informed that, on and after

MONDAY, THE 19th MARCH,

The above COACH will leave

BERWICK every Morning, (Sundays excepted,) at Six o'Clock,

Belford, at a Quarter before Eight,

And, after Breakfasting at Alnwick, will leave at 10 o'Clock,

And arrive at

MR. DODSWORTH'S,

QUEEN'S HEAD, NEWCASTLE, AT TWO O'CLOCK;

And leave the Queen's Head, Newcastle, at ½-past 11 o'Clock, A.M;

AND AFTER DINING AT ALNWICK,

Will leave at Four o'Clock,

And arrive at Berwick at 8 o'Clock.

Fares from Newcastle to Berwick, 13s. Insides, 7s. Outside.
Do.   Do.   to Alnwick, 7s.   Do.   4s. Do.

CHARLES HENRY COOK PRINTER PILGRIM STREET NEWCASTLE

4. HOW IT ALL BEGAN

Generally accepted as the first 'bus' was George Shillibeer's horse-drawn bus in London in 1829. He began a regular service with fares within the means of more of the people. For want of a better name he called it an 'Omnibus', the Latin word meaning 'for all', and the name stuck. Being a compact town, Berwick had no need of omnibuses at that time. People continued to walk or use carriers. In the second part of the 19th century 'omnibuses' began to appear in the town. Adverts for the King's Arms and for the then Red Lion in High Street said that 'omnibuses met all trains at Berwick Station'.

The annual Sunday school trips and other private parties could hire horse-drawn wagonettes or, if you were really well off, there were hansom cabs for hire. Their stand was at Berwick's Town Hall steps with the cabin used by the drivers appearing on old photos of the High Street.

Motorbuses began to appear about 1900. They were primitive

vehicles with solid tyres, chain-driven, just a flat body with rows of hard seats screwed to it. They offered minimal protection in inclement weather. Many were used as lorries during the week, with seats fitted for the weekend.

The passengers all wore hats, the womens with big brims tied down with scarves. 'Charabancs' were soon developed; in their early days much more comfortable than the flat trucks. They had rows of seats with doors at the end of each row and a folding canvas hood for bad weather. The bodies were high off the ground with guard slats along the sides to prevent animals and small children from straying underneath. There were also a few double-deckers, all open-topped, in some places but not in Berwick.

Berwick town's first was one of these 'charabancs.' It was an '18/25 hp Commer motor car, with charabanc body, French grey, 2 tons 10cwts, for public conveyance.' It was registered on 31st July 1913. Seahouses had a motorbus ten years earlier. There is more about both in subsequent chapters.

What might not be realised is the impact motor vehicles had on the roads. Road surfaces were less than brilliant and were churned up by the solid tyres. People just wandered on the carriageway; children played there, and road safety had to be taught.

5. BEFORE THE INTERNAL COMBUSTION ENGINE

Not a lot to do with buses but people still had to travel so how did they go?

By the early 19th century if you had a long way to go, for example to London, ships made the trip frequently and on an (almost) regular timetable. The famous 'Berwick smacks' took you to London for about £1.00 single and were 'well armed.'

By 1823 the London & Edinburgh Steam Packet Co., and these were very early steamships, would take you to London or to Newhaven (Edinburgh) weekly. The fare from Berwick to London was four times that of the smacks and there was another disadvantage. Their boats did not come into the river, but remained off the Pier. Intending passengers had to wait until the packet boat came into sight then go out in small boats and be transferred - off the Pier - to the Company's 'elegant' steamboats.

By road, the first mail coach ran on 7th November 1786 from Edinburgh to London via Berwick. It travelled at 7mph, or two hours per stage, a stage being Berwick-Belford; Belford-Alnwick, etc. It carried letters and newspapers, and four passengers, 'none on top', at a fare of 6d per mile. On these, too, the guard was stated to be 'well-armed.'

That was not necessarily the first coach, as a London-Edinburgh coach was reported to be running in 1763. It ran only once a month, taking two weeks for the journey.

This was the era of the stagecoach. In 1800, the 'Union' coach ran a similar service as the mail coach. It carried 10 passengers, some 'outside.' The fare was reduced to 4d per mile if you travelled outside.

The 'New Royal Charlotte' coach between Edinburgh, Berwick and Newcastle, making a connection at Newcastle into the 'Royal Charlotte' for London, was advertised in 1809. The fare to London was then £6.35 inside, or £4.25 outside. Compare that with the Berwick smacks at £1.00. single.

By about 1830 stagecoaches were running between London and Edinburgh via Morpeth, Wooler, and Coldstream. The Tankerville Arms at Wooler was a staging post on this route.

On the Berwick route meal stops of half an hour were made at either the King's Arms, the Red Lion, or the Hen and Chickens. Some of the coach crews lived in Berwick, including the Surveyor of Mail Coaches, a Mr. William Gibson.

There were various local stagecoach services. The 'Border Union' ran between Berwick and Kelso two or three times a week; the 'Regulator' ran between Berwick and Dunse(sic); the 'Defence' and the 'Despatch' between Berwick and Alnwick; and the 'Cheviot' from Wooler to Berwick and return on Saturdays. These were running by the late 1820s.The heyday of the stagecoach was to be short-lived, most disappearing with the advent of railways; that from Edinburgh to Berwick on 22nd June 1846, and from Newcastle to Tweedmouth in July 1847. The Royal Border Bridge opened in August 1849 although a temporary bridge had been in use since October 1848. Just how quick the demise of stagecoaches was is illustrated by the auction of coaches and 20 horses on 4th July 1846 by John Bird of Houndwood. The last mail coach left Berwick on 5th July 1847 as mails were then going by train.

With the opening of the Kelso branch line in 1849, that stagecoach service went, too. An auction in Berwick in August 1850 sold off various vehicles from that road, the largest having room for 18 passengers.

Where no railways existed, coaches continued to run, indeed new services were started. The Newcastle Chronicle records in 1860 the introduction of a coach service from Wooler to Alnwick by Mr.Sinclair of the Black Bull, Wooler. It carried mails and passengers. Mr.Sinclair had introduced a mail coach, the 'Alma', between Wooler and Coldstream in 1855. Another ran at 10.0am daily from the Black Bull, Wooler to the Blue Bell, Belford, returning at 3.15pm. Mrs.McGregor ran that one.

The longest lasting stagecoach goes to the 'Cheviot' from Wooler to Berwick on Saturdays. It was running in 1834 from the Sun Inn at Wooler, then occupied by Andrew Fairnington, surviving until the railway between Alnwick, Wooler and Coldstream opened in 1887. James Henderson, Mrs.Eleanor Fairnington, and Selby Fairnington are also noted as running that coach at some time.

The railways killed the long stagecoach services but created a demand for connections to railway stations by horse 'omnibuses'. In 1847, with the opening of the Newcastle-Tweedmouth railway but without the Royal Border Bridge having been opened, passengers travelling across Berwick had to be transferred by omnibus between the stations for which 40 minutes was allowed. Cattle taken by train had to be driven between the stations across the Old Bridge and up the narrow streets by those we know in Berwick as 'bullock wallopers.'

'Omnibuses' were arranged to connect with principal trains at many stations. The North British Railway arranged for one to run between Duns and Reston Station until the Duns branch opened in 1849. Similarly, they were run between North Sunderland and Chathill and between Bamburgh and Lucker.

'LOWICK JIMMY.'

Transport has always had its eccentrics and the Wooler coach bred one of them, 'Lowick Jimmy.'

James Murray was born in Lowick about 1860. Censuses quote him as a labourer but he was a wanderer. He was said to have a constitution of steel. No Hirings or Fair were complete without him. One of his feats of endurance was to race the stagecoach which ran between Wooler and Berwick before the railway opened. This coach ran then from Bertram's in Wooler and Jimmy boasted he could beat it every time. He ran barefoot, boots and socks round his neck, resting only at Doddington, Redscar, or at the pub at Biteabout. People in the coach would throw him money and, to finish, he would spurt up Wooler or Berwick High Street shouting 'victory', roaring, and foaming at the mouth. He would race alongside any pony and trap if he thought he would get a copper or two. What he earned was spent on liquid refreshment.

The leader in the 'Berwickshire News' of 31st December 1895 is headed 'Berwick's Worthies'. It reads, 'the 21st appearance at Berwick Police Court of James Murray - Lowick Jimmy - reminds us that though Berwick still has her 'Worthies', they are neither so numerous nor so pronounced as they were some twenty or thirty years ago. Lowick Jimmy certainly belongs to the category of present day 'Border Worthies.' He is a native of Lowick; and he first came into prominence at Berwick by his weekly feat - performed every Saturday - of running into Berwick alongside the Wooler coach. And proud he was of his performance! With the opening of the Alnwick and Cornhill Railway, the Wooler Coach went the way of the old Stage Coaches; still, Lowick Jimmy has managed to be at Berwick pretty often - perchance too often. This man is particularly eccentric but he is not perhaps sufficiently so to obtain his removal to a place of safety. At the same time, not much, if any, good is attained by sending the poor fellow to prison for a few days. His is a case for compulsory detention in some suitable institution for a prolonged period.'

So much for the social history. Jimmy was taken into the workhouse but wanted to remain in the open. He was eventually found by the roadside near Duddo and taken to the workhouse for the last time. He was over seventy when he died.

For those who could not afford the stagecoach and that was most country people, there was always the local carrier.

Carriers had always served villages and, while mainly there to carry goods, they would take the odd passenger - as long as they could tolerate a slow journey. They provided a network of services, local and long distance, running on specified days and times from one of the local pubs. The coastal area between Berwick and Alnmouth was particularly well served. Pigot & Co.'s National Commercial Directory for 1834 lists them all. Berwick had 21 destinations listed, some served by more than one carrier; Alnwick had 40 destinations. An earlier directory, that of 1806, showed a carrier from Berwick to Dumfries.

Wooler, too, had its own carriers. Of Thomas and Henry Howey it was said, in 1828, that 'they were the first to start 'well-regulated waggons instead of pack horses.'

ABOUT THE ROADS

Having talked a bit about horse transport from about 1800, what about the roads? Responsibility for roads lay originally with the King, the Monasteries, or with the Lord of the Manor. Turnpike roads, for which a toll had to be paid, came in the first instance in 1663, when the Great North Road was created. Turnpike Trusts, with tollgates at specified points, were set up. From about 1800 it seems that things began to be a bit better regulated. Berwick had Turnpike Trusts whose Minutes for the period 1819-1846 are held by Berwick Record Office.

An Act of Parliament of 1831 consolidated trusts in the Wooler area, becoming known as the 'Wooler Turnpike Roads.' Another Act, of 1861, deals with the 'Berwick, Norham and Islandshire Trust.' The book, 'Wooler and Glendale - a Brief History', volume 1, published in 1986 by the Glendale Local History Society, gives much interesting information on the terms of that Act. Tollgates were auctioned to the highest bidder.

An Act of 1855 placed the responsibility for road maintenance with individual parishes. It obliged parishioners to spend prescribed days per year working on the roads, bringing with them their own tools, horses and carts.

By about 1880 the Turnpike Trusts had disappeared after legislation had set up local bodies capable of maintaining the roads themselves.

HORSE TRAMWAYS.

These tend to be seen as something in cities in the mid to late 19C. Rudimentary tramways were developed long before that. There was a waggonway from Unthank Colliery to Tweedmouth by 1764, and another ran down Spittal Main Street in 1821, built to carry stone from Hud's Head Quarries for the building of Berwick Pier. It was used afterwards to carry coal from Scremerston Colliery.

A more sophisticated public horse tramway was planned to operate between Tweedmouth and Kelso by an Act of Parliament of 1811. There were legal difficulties related to the then County Palatine of Durham, i.e. Norham and Islandshire. Not enough capital was forthcoming and the scheme was abandoned in 1827 but revived in 1836 when the projected cost was £100,000. Once again capital was not found and, by 1844, the idea of a branch line along the Tweed connecting with the proposed Newcastle-Berwick railway overtook any further thought of a tramway. The railway branch line from Tweedmouth to Sprouston opened in July 1849, being extended to Kelso in 1851.

THE LAST DAYS OF HORSE BUSES

We have seen that many stagecoaches finished with the advent of railways except to places where the railways had not reached. The railways themselves had generated a need for services to link them with towns and large villages where stations were absent or not conveniently situated. Thus horse buses, or more correctly, omnibuses, were still in favour. Few records exist about them but some information can be gleaned from directories. In general they carried about 15 passengers.

In Berwick, omnibuses from the Red Lion met all trains at Berwick Station. The King's Arms did better than that. Edward Davidson's bus met every train at Berwick Station from its opening for passengers to and from the King's Arms. He gave a similar service to and from Tweedmouth Station to connect with Newcastle trains until the two stations were linked, after which he continued to serve Berwick Station. They were still operating in the early part of the 20C.

In WOOLER, the Black Bull had its own coach, which took its guests to and from Wooler

'Sandy's bus' on its way back to Coldstream from the station at Cornhill. The house on the left is the former Toll House, busier as a Marriage House in its day than Gretna Green. *(R.L.Grieves)*

A 1925 classic at Kelso Station. The Chevrolet bus, KS 2555, belongs to the Cross Keys Hotel. Its driver is Arthur Scott. The horse-drawn coach, with coachman Dick Scott, is going to the Queen's Head.

Station until the railway closed in 1930. James Thompson was the long-term driver.

In COLDSTREAM, they had Sandy's bus to take passengers to and from the station at Cornhill - and hear the local gossip. James Ford was the local 'post horse and carriage hirer.'

BELFORD had an omnibus service between the Blue Bell and the station and, going just outside the Borough, Mr.Foggan of GLANTON had a brake, in effect a posh horse and cart, to meet trains there when required. Bamburgh, Seahouses and other places had them, too.

For outings there were brakes and wagonettes and, for the inevitable Sunday school picnic, they used horses and carts.

6. MOTOR VEHICLES ARRIVE

Near the end of the 19C the first motor vehicles appeared. Their development was rapid after having been hindered for some years by the so-called Red Flag Act - the Locomotive Act of 1865. Requiring a man with a red flag to precede a motor vehicle, the new inventions could barely compete with the horse. The earliest motoring offence I can find was reported in the 'Berwick Journal' of 19th March 1896 when Mr.T.R.B.Elliot, of Clifton Park, Morebattle was apprehended in Bridge Street, Berwick at 2.45 one morning driving without a 'red flag' man. He had driven from Morebattle. He was fined 6d with 19/7d costs. The Act was repealed in 1896 allowing a speed limit of 12 mph on these 'horseless carriages.' Thus the door was opened to motor buses and the first officially licensed bus service started in 1898. It ran in Edinburgh between the Post Office and the Haymarket using a Milnes-Daimler motor wagonette.

The Motor Car Act of 1903 increased the maximum speed for vehicles of under 3 tons to 20 mph, although a Local Government Board could reduce that to 10 mph. The 1903 Act also required vehicles to be registered and drivers to be licensed. The first number plates were issued from 1st January 1904, the prefix letter for Northumberland being 'X'.

The Heavy Motor Car Order of 1904 raised the unladen weight to 5 tons with a maximum speed of 12 mph provided that all wheels were fitted with rubber tyres. By rubber tyres it meant solid rubber tyres as pneumatic tyres had not been invented. The 'horseless carriages' gave the local jokers their chances. One such went round Lowick telling everybody that 'there is a horseless carriage in....'s yard.' Along went the excited gullibles to find, yes, there was a horse-less carriage there, but it was an ordinary cart uncoupled from its horse!

7. THE FIRST BUS SERVICES IN BERWICK

Credit belongs to S.E.CUTHBERTSON of Seahouses for this. The North Sunderland Railway opened to passenger traffic in 1898. Their timetable for 1899 shows connections with trains at Seahouses Station to and from Bamburgh by horse bus. The 'Berwick Advertiser' of the day reported that agreement had been reached between Cuthbertson and the Railway Company to provide this service. Not only was it a first bus service, but also a first for road/rail integration. It would be many years before another road/rail scheme would appear i.e. the Borders Link between Berwick and Galashiels. The horse bus service continued until 1st April 1905 when CUTHBERTSON bought the first motor wagonette, of unknown manufacture, but registered X 482. A second one, X 958, was bought in 1907. Nothing more is known about their activities at this period and these buses are unlikely to have survived in the 1914-18 War. Cuthbertsons had a garage, the Castle Garage, in Seahouses. At some time after 1918 they acquired a charabanc. It does not seem to have been run on a timetabled service, just on tours and private hires. This garage was badly damaged by fire and the charabanc may have been damaged or destroyed then. The surviving part was sold to Bolton Bros., of whom more later.

BERWICK-UPON-TWEED MOTOR CAR CO. LTD.

What I regard as the first service in Berwick itself was when the Berwick-upon-Tweed Motor Car Co.Ltd. was formed in 1913, with its Registered Office at the Quayside.

The Directors were: -

    Adam Logan, Corn Merchant,
    William Cowe Richardson, Gentleman,
    William Wood, Hotel Keeper,
    Samuel Oliphant, Confectioner.

Authorised capital was £2500 and the Company Secretary was John Logan.

The 'Berwick Journal' reported: - 'the new motor charabanc, secured for Berwick through the enterprise of the Mayor, began its series of tours yesterday afternoon, when a fairly large company took advantage of the run to Norham

Adam Logan (right) and John Logan (left) gently touch their 'comfortably fitted out' Commer charabanc, KS 99, about to depart on its first outing to Bamburgh at 10am on 1st August 1913. This was Berwick town's first bus, owned by the Berwick upon Tweed Motor Car Co. Ltd. It stands in Sandgate outside the Corn Exchange. The well-heeled passengers paid four shillings for the outing - a week's rent for many at the time.

and Ladykirk. The vehicle, which is comfortably fitted up, should prove a popular attraction next week when the Border Holidays are on.'

The 'new motor charabanc' was registered on 31st July 1913 as an '18/25 hp Commer motor car; charabanc; colour - French grey; weight 2 tons 10 cwts; for public conveyance' by John Logan, 47, Church Street, Berwick. Its registration number was KS 99, a number previously held by a lorry belonging to Logans, whose premises were along Ness Street, Berwick.

Mrs. Mosgrove, one of the Logan family, told me that Adam Logan himself drove the bus to Berwick from the factory, then at Luton. With a maximum speed of 12 mph, this was no mean feat. It went straight into use, the 'Berwick Journal' carrying an advertisement: -

**For hire by day or hour an up-to-date motor charabanc
Leaving from the Alnwick & Berwick Garage, Hide Hill, the above will,**

weather permitting, run as follows:

**Friday 1st August
Trip to Bamburgh, leaving at 10 am, return at 7 pm.
Fare: 4/-**

**Saturday 2nd August
Trips round Chain Bridge, leaving at 12 noon; 2 pm; 4 pm.
Fare: 1/-**

**Monday 4th August (August Bank Holiday)
Trip to North Berwick, leaving at 10 am, return about 7 pm.
Fare: 5/-
'Book seats early.'
'Parties wishing to hire the above should apply at once to John Logan.'**

Further trips were advertised to Kelso Show to Duns; and to Dunbar that week.

More trips were advertised for the following week but also, on 7th August, the advertisement read: -

See posters for motor charabanc service between Berwick and Spittal.

There are no details of this Spittal service but it seems to have been evenings only. It certainly was a service as weekly tickets were available.

Adam Logan was the entrepreneur of his day with interests in shipping, coal, and fuel as well as being the Norwegian Consul. He owned the Berwick-Spittal ferry for some time, buying it when Mr.Thomas Elliott, 'Stapper Tammy', retired, and selling it on to the Spowart brothers. He died in 1923 while on holiday in Bergen, Norway.

William Cowe Richardson was a Berwick man who became a glove manufacturer in London. His business was very successful and, having sold out to Dents, he retired to Berwick at a comparatively early age.

William Wood ran Wood's Hotel in Berwick's High Street and the family ran Wood's Club, a local savings club.

Samuel Oliphant was a confectioner with a shop in High Street. He was before my time but I have a particular memory of him. He had owned a picture with moving parts, showing a drunk man trying, and failing, to get his door key into the lock, whilst above, his wife leant out of the window brandishing a rolling pin. That picture passed to Mrs.Ritchie who displayed it in her shop window at 22, West Street every Christmas. As children we used to stand for hours waiting to see if he could get the key into the keyhole.

So, with Adam Logan's bus advertising a service to Spittal, it must be the first true service in the town.

We have to move now to 1920 for the next known buses. As already mentioned, information is very sketchy and there may be omissions but, to my knowledge, the first to run after the 1914-18 War was JAMES WHILLIS, Coxon's Lane and College Place, Berwick.

JAMES WHILLIS AND SONS.

James Whillis started in 1912 as a Haulage Contractor with one motor lorry. 'They did anything that needed moving', Bobby Whillis, son of the founder, told me. Their lorry was garaged first at Berwick Quayside, then later in Ness Street where Cleet Court now stands. In 1921 they moved to Coxon's Lane and bought a second vehicle, a wartime surplus Pierce-Arrow. This was from a quality American car maker who added trucks to its production in 1910. Whillis bought more lorries and, eventually, a charabanc body. Every Friday night Mr. & Mrs.Whillis unbolted a lorry body from its chassis and fitted the charabanc body for the weekend. The process had to be reversed for Monday morning. They took private parties or did trips locally but no services were run. The most popular trips were Sunday afternoons to Ford and Etal; to Wooler; or to Coldstream, getting back about 6 pm. 'They had leather covers if the weather turned nasty.'

By 1924 Whillis had three Thornycroft charabancs and later a small Chevrolet, expanding the tours and outings part of the business. Mr.Whillis ceased to operate the charas by 1930 but retained the Chevrolet until 1935, concentrating on his haulage business. The firm was nationalised in 1945, becoming a unit of British Road Services. It was returned to private ownership in 1955, continuing until 1983 when ill health forced closure.

Bobby Whillis told me about the solid tyres fitted to their charabancs before the development of pneumatic tyres. Although made from rubber, the solid tyres had no capacity to react to temperature changes. After running for some time the rubber expanded with heat and friction and the tyres were liable to fall off. The drivers carried sacking and when this happened they wrapped sacking round the tyres and refitted them. Seemingly all in a day's work!

S.E.YOUNG

Around the same time as Whillis had his charabancs Spittal had a charabanc owner - Samuel Young, whose garage was at 3, Main Street. No details have come to light about his bus and it is likely it was used for outings. Young had a licence to store petrol in 1921 - as had Whillis and others at the time - and he sold cars. In 1923 he was advertising Buick and Crossley cars and a Chevrolet van for sale.

Time has moved on to the early 1920s and sees the start of bus services in earnest. In Berwick itself came Thompson, Spowart and J W Young with more than just outings. This had become the time for 'real' bus services - regular, and running to timetables. But more than that, these were the years of competition.

8. THE TRANSPORT EXPLOSION - COMPETITION AND PIRACY

From 1919 the concept of running buses on a regular service caught on and now the Borough would see these developed everywhere.

Lack of records and the lack of an efficient licensing system in the smaller towns means that one cannot be certain when individual bus operators set up in business or where exactly they ran. Others ran what they thought was required for local communities in the way of buses to markets and events.

It goes without saying that the 1914-18 War changed the world. Attitudes had changed. There was a huge surplus of ex-Army vehicles available from auctions at knock-down prices. Men had left the Forces with skills in motor engineering and were seeking jobs, and had gratuities to invest in their own businesses. Many did not want to return to jobs in industry where conditions had been bad. They saw transport as a means of being independent. The army vehicles were lorries but they could be adapted easily to carry passengers, or be used as convertible vehicles - goods during the week, buses at weekends. They were technically advanced on those of 1913 and there were unfulfilled transport needs.

The railways had built up a coarse transport network across the country before 1914 and some railway companies, the North Eastern one of them, had begun to develop their own bus services as a means of providing feeder services to their stations - and to ward off potential calls for new railway lines.

Manufacturers, having opened production lines for wartime needs, wanted to keep them open and were prepared to offer favourable terms to buyers.

Many municipalities, and some companies, had been running electric trams for forty years; some had begun to develop bus services, too. What was there to stop me from running a bus

service? - not a lot!

What was it like to run buses in the 1920s?

It would be nice to be able to talk with some of the early entrepreneurs. That has been left too late but I have been able to talk with and, in some cases, record some of the 'survivors'.

CLYDESDALE'S BUSES

In 1998 I was fortunate to record Mr.Ralph Clydesdale's memories on tape. Born in Chopwell in 1907 and living in Berwick, he had a story to tell. It does not describe what happened in the Berwick area but in Chopwell, Co.Durham, roughly between Newcastle and Consett.

About the turn of the century, his mother, as well as bringing up a young family, decided to set up in business as a carrier, with a horse and cart, in Chopwell. The business prospered and by 1914 Mrs.Clydesdale had a number of horses and carts and a hearse - and employment for the family. She kept the business going through the 1914-18 War. About 1920 she saw the writing on the wall, auctioned the carts, put the horses to graze, and started to buy motor vehicles. First she bought two ex-army convertibles, a Leyland and an AEC. They served as goods vehicles during the week and buses at the weekends. Their regular Saturday job was to carry Chopwell Colliery Band and to serve football matches. She then bought two 14 seater Fiat buses and a Darracq car, modified to carry goods. With the Fiats she started bus services from Chopwell to Newcastle and to Consett.

Mrs.Clydesdale continued to buy buses- a Delauney-Belleville in 1923; an AEC in 1925; a De Dion in 1926; ADCs in 1926 and 1927; and an Albion in 1929, and for which she converted the former stables to a bus garage.

Ralph described how all the family worked in the business. He left school at 14 and became a conductor. He had a motorbike licence at 14, too. 'There was no test - I just applied for it and got it.' 'I got a car licence at 16 by chance. I had applied for a renewal for the motor bike, but failed to cross out 'motor car' on the application, so I was given a car licence.

'I went bus driving then. I was twice picked up for speeding, both times at 23 mph, once at Scotswood when I was fined £5.00, and once at Highgate, London, when the fine was £2.00.'

By 1926 there was competition on their routes from J&M Parker of Chopwell; Robson Bros., of High Spen; and Mrs.Amy Bessford, of High Spen. They survived the competition until Mrs.Clydesdale again saw the writing on the wall in the form of the 1930 Road Traffic Act and sold out to Reed Bros., later Venture, in late 1930. Ralph died in late 1999.

The Clydesdale story is only one of very many. Many of these 'small men' ran in cut-throat competition with one another. The buses themselves were pushed hard and corners were cut on maintenance.

A very young Ralph Clydesdale stands in front of his De Dion 18-seater, PT 7491, in Newcastle, waiting to depart on the family's bus service to Chopwell. No destination blind, one small mirror and two midget side lamps.

Garages might well be wooden sheds within which petrol and oil were spilt making them fire traps. Insurance was not always taken so if there was a fire then their livelihood was lost overnight. If money was not being made in one place they went somewhere else, creating, in some places, sheer piracy.

So, on 1st January 1931, the 1930 Road Traffic Act brought about much needed regulation through the licensing of routes, vehicles, drivers, conductors as well as setting out proper standards of maintenance through Certificates of Fitness for vehicles.

9. REGULAR BUS SERVICES COME TO BERWICK TOWN

By the early 1920s changes were well under way. Buses were not just for outings. In some respects Berwick was a little late in getting 'regular' bus services. It had a main railway station with good passenger services. Seahouses, Norham, Cornhill and Wooler all had railway stations. But larger villages like Lowick had no regular transport and, in the town itself, potential was seen for buses to Spittal, more convenient than the ferry. Thus in 1923 the first local men to run regular bus services began - Thompson, Spowart, and John Young. (John Young has no connection with the S.E.Young of Spittal who never ran a bus service as such).

When they actually started their services is not recorded, the licensing system being very sketchy at that time. The only reasonably reliable guide comes from vehicle registrations. Taking that line, then THOMPSON BROS. were first.

The brothers, Robert, Andrew, and Hector established a haulage business in 1912. They ran both steam and motor wagons, building up a considerable business before buying their first bus, NL 4614, a 16-seater Albion, in March 1923. Just where they began is uncertain, possibly between Scremerston and Berwick, but it was not long before they were running between Berwick and Spittal, and that may have been before Spowart.

No doubt the venture was a success as they bought a second Albion, a 20 seater, in June 1924. Three more buses were bought, in 1927, 1928 and 1931. Trade had taken off as the first two of those were 26 and 25 seaters. The last one, in 1931, was a 14 seater, bought specifically to meet the restrictions then placed on bus size on the Old Bridge.

Most bus operators give their buses an individual fleet number. Thompson did something very unusual, and probably unique in the industry, in identifying his five buses with the names of the first five letters of the Greek

Thompson's Albion PJ26, TY 4174, new in 1928, stands at Belford. The driver is Norman Inglis.

A fine array of Spowart Bros. buses at Berwick Quayside on Whit Sunday 1933. Nearest the camera is UP 2788, a Guy ex-Parker, Rowlands Gill. Second from the left is Jimmy Baxter, later an Inspector with United.

alphabet: - Alpha, Beta, Gamma, Delta, and Epsilon (sic).

As well as the Spittal and Scremerston services, Thompsons introduced services from Berwick to Branxton via Ford, and a summer service from Berwick to Philadelphia, better known to us as Cocklawburn. He also ran to Spittal via the New Bridge after it opened in 1930. As well as those, he retained a programme of tours and outings advertised in the local papers weekly.

Thompson's service to Philadelphia is

interesting. United took it over in 1934 and ran it as service 69 until 1939, on Thursday and Sunday afternoons. The terminal in the timetable is 'The Café.' It is hard to imagine how buses ever turned at Cocklawburn as space was very limited and, even with short buses, drivers had to make several cuts to get round.

Thompson Bros., who traded from No. 3 Main Street, Spittal, sold their bus business to United in 1934. Some of the staff transferred on a full or part time basis, including John Richardson, Bob Blaikie, Pat Fitzgerald, and Markie Thompson. Others on his staff were R.Ambrose, J.Brown, J.Inglis, A.Learmonth, R.Leith, and R.Weymes. Their buses were green with a black top. Robert Thompson, one of the sons, and the mainstay of the bus business, was also a cyclist of note, being an Olympic Gold Medallist in his sport.

The idea of Thompson having started a bus service to Spittal could not have gone down well with SPOWART BROS. They had the Spittal ferry, of which more in another chapter, and therefore the monopoly of the passengers.

They bought their first bus, NL 4905, an 18 seater GMC, in May 1923 for the Spittal service. From then on there was intensive rivalry between Spowart and Thompson. As it was so indicative of the cut-throat competition of the 1920s, I have looked at the operation in some detail and given it a chapter of its own.

The GMC bus, NL 4905, was indeed a General Motors product. The firm was American, formed in 1911 by the merger of two lorry manufacturers. Their buses were mainly around the 20 seater mark and not common in Britain. It seems to have been an unusual choice. Nevertheless it proved so successful that, two months later, in July 1923, they bought a second bus, a 20 seater Karrier. Between 1923 and 1931 another seven buses were bought, being Reo, more GMC, Chevrolet and Bedford. With the exception of two 20 seaters, all were small 14 seaters, in latter days some were bought second hand. Their red painted buses were easily distinguished from Thompsons, and return tickets were available on either bus or ferry.

As their bus fleet expanded Spowart leased premises on Berwick Quayside, previously occupied by the Pinkston Oil Company, from the Harbour Commissioners. United did not renew the lease after its expiry in November 1934, nine months after take over.

As well as the original route to Spittal, Spowart had services from Berwick to Lowick; to Shoreswood; to Crookham Westfield; to Fenton, and a Ford circular route. He, too, ran to Spittal via the New Bridge from 1930. 1934 saw him sell out to United although he continued to run the Spittal ferry until 1939.

Spowarts' staff included T.G.Allan, Jimmy Baxter, Jack Todd, his engineer, Albert Todd, Jackie Hay, Jack Oliver, G.Gauntlett, W.Hardy, M.Henderby, A.Jefferson, D.McAllister, R.Patterson, R.Veale, and H.Wilson. .

The Spowart family were well known in the town. Philip Spowart, who looked after the bus business, was Mayor of Berwick in the 1930s. His brother, Robert, looked after the ferries. He had served his time as a sail maker and had a lifetime interest in sailing.

The third member of this trio of bus operators is JOHN W.YOUNG.

John Young was one of a farming family from Norham. He did not want to stay in farming and decided to buy a bus, a 14 seater convertible lorry/bus, in 1923. His first bus was an 18 seater Albion charabanc, NL 7137, in 1924. He bought a small bus, a 14 or 20 seater, each year until 1928 by which time passenger traffic must have been looking up, as he bought bigger buses, with 26-32 seats, and of Guy, Albion or Gilford make. By 1932 he was running seven buses in maroon livery from his garage in Castle Street, Norham, between Norham and Berwick and Berwick and Wooler. He had the odd Saturday journey between Berwick and Chatton, and between Berwick and Lowick via Ford. John Young's Gilford bus was one of the 1680T types, popular with independent operators around 1930. The Gilfords were good buses - his went first to United, moving on to four other operators, and surviving until December 1950. He was fortunate, too, in having little competition with his services, only that between Berwick and Lowick. Little has survived of his timetables; the only copy found being in Reid's Railway Guide of the day.

John Young was the first of the three to sell out to United. His agreement to sell is dated 24th October 1933; Thompson and Spowart signed up on 1st November 1933. United bought only the Norham and Wooler services and his five newest buses for which they paid £5000. As with the other two, John Young was debarred from

Above: John W.Young's Gilford 168OT, TY 9490, taken at Norham c.1932. From the right - Jimmy Todd, Ralph Swan, Aaron Oliver, John Young, J.Hume, Janet Jobson, Carmichael, unidentified, Andy Murray, J.Welsh, unidentified, unidentified. The staff are in uniform, unusual for a small operator.

Below: Leyland LT1 Lion TY6217, United's LT4-10, at Wooler c.1936. The bus was new to T.Allen, Blyth, passing to United as AL251, later renumbered in the LT class. It was allocated to Yetholm outstation to work services 67 and 71. From the left: unidentified, unidentified, Jimmy Todd, Markie Thompson, unidentified, Jimmy Wilson. It was this bus whose starting handle nearly decapitated Jimmy Todd.

operating, directly or indirectly, any buses within Northumberland or Durham for three years from take over. In fact he came with the buses, becoming United's first Local Traffic Superintendent at Berwick, a post he held until resigning in 1946. He went on to buy a Rolls Royce to run a taxi service in Berwick where he was a well-known local figure. He died in 1990 aged 95.

Most, or all, of his staff came to United with him. They included Andy Murray, Ralph Swan, John Garland, Jimmy Todd, Aaron Oliver, Janet Jobson, J.Welsh and M.Oliver. Ralph Swan went into business on his own account in 1950 with a new Commer coach. His son carries on the business and operates most of the Berwick-Norham service.

Another irrelevant snippet concerns John Young's Rolls Royce, which had a high clearance from the road. Within Berwick's Walls are no crossroads. The layout for defence was to have staggered junctions. One snowy winter's day, a girl was sledging down Ravensdowne, a hill leading to the staggered junction at Silver Street/Ness Street. As John Young drove across the junction, the girl and the sledge came flying down at right angles. The sledge, and passenger, went right underneath the moving taxi and out the other side. She never had a scratch! No names, etc.!

Another private operator to succumb was JOHN STENHOUSE, Town Yetholm.

He began in the early 1920s with a 14 seater Albion carrying schoolchildren from Sourhope to Yetholm School. In due course he began a Yetholm-Kelso service, later extended to Jedburgh; a Yetholm-Wooler; and a Yetholm-Berwick. He sold his bus services in 1934, part to United and part to SMT, the latter taking the Kelso service, which still operates. United took over the Town Yetholm-Berwick service on 30th October 1934, at the same time withdrawing their Berwick-Ford-Branxton service. United and SMT each took two buses. Initially, United operated the Berwick service from their Wooler premises. It took a circuitous route, starting at Town Yetholm and going via Mindrum, Akeld, Wooler; back to Akeld, then via Branxton and Ford to Berwick. Some journeys took three hours, including a break in Wooler. At that time the fare for the full journey was 2/9 single, 5/- return. To put the fares in context, we lived in a small apartment in West Street, Berwick for which we paid 4/- per week. By the summer of 1936, perhaps earlier, the service was extended to start from Kirk Yetholm taking a more direct route from Mindrum to Berwick via either Milfield or Branxton. That reduced the journey time and the fare.

<< *Previous page:* **An advertisement from the local newspaper dated 5th July 1928.**

Above: **Lancia charabanc ES 6606 of Redfearn, Berwick, new in 1924, leads the pair. The driver is Joe White. Behind is the Thompson Bros. Albion NL 7458, new in the same year. This vehicle passed to Lowson, Kirriemuir, who had a bus body fitted, and then to SMT as fleet number A110. Mr Brown sent this photograph to John Richardson, Thompson's driver "when you drove us to Eyemouth, etc., on the occasion of our trip to Berwick on 6th June 1925."**

Stenhouse's sale was different from the others, perhaps because it was a joint sale to United and SMT. They did not buy the goodwill of his services. The two companies also had the right to continue to run Stenhouse's four buses under the Stenhouse name if they wished. United's publicity suggests they, at least, did not. The agreement allowed Stenhouse to hire motorcars for small private parties not exceeding six persons, but not for ten years as hire cars on the regular routes of the purchasers - so he could not take people to Kelso. For hires, the purchase agreements laid down what Stenhouse could charge. The exclusion clause in his case was more severe than that of Spowart, etc., in that he could not operate, manage, etc., any interest in competition with United/SMT within a radius of sixty miles from Yetholm Post Office for a period of ten years.

United set up an out-station at Yetholm from which the Berwick service (Service 67) and part of the Wooler service (Service 71) operated. Three United staff were kept at Yetholm; a driver, a conductor, and a driver/conductor. They included George Faulder, Sid Lunn, Jimmy

Todd, formerly with Young at Norham, and either Jack Robson or Eddie Unwin. Operation there was hardly profitable. Staff paid the takings in at Berwick - a day's work might yield 1/4d.

John Stenhouse had Willie Watson as mechanic. The only known conductress was Maisie Hogarth who later worked for the SMT at Kelso for many years. He also employed Richie Stenhouse as a driver/conductor (no relation, incidentally), Richie going to SMT and working from their Yetholm out-station.

The Wooler -Yetholm service, 71, was useful for the country folk. Tommy Oliver was the shepherd at Fleehope, in the College Valley. When he needed to go to Wooler the choice was to walk eleven miles 'over the hill' or five miles down the valley to Westnewton where he could catch Service 71. Tommy was in Wooler on a shopping foray, his last call was to buy a mouse trap. Bella McEwan had a hardware shop. An Aladdin's cave, she sold everything. To say she was slow was an underestimation. As the bus departure rushed nearer, Tommy became alarmed. 'Hurry up, Miss McEwan, hev ye' go

Above: "It was a funny looking bus, everybody came out to see it." Cuthbertson's charabanc on an outing from Beadnell in the early 1920s.

Below: The only known photograph of Rutherford's buses is this late 1920s postcard of Craster. The bus is thought to be a Gilford, CN 3496 or CN 3669. From here, too, Adam Archbold ran his 'Ocean Maid' to Little Mill Station. Craster is also famed for kippers! *(R.C.Davis)*

that moose trap, ah hev a bus te' catch.' Deadly serious came a voice from the back, 'Ay, Mister Oliver, ah divvent sell moose traps te' catch buses!'

One busman who survived further into the 1930s was DAVID REDFEARN, Golden Square, Berwick. Unlike Thompson, Spowart and Young, he never ran any 'proper' bus services, but he did have a contract between Berwick and Longridge Towers School. His main activity was excursions and tours. He began sometime in the early 1920s when Golden Square was not the Berwick entrance to the Royal Tweed Bridge, but one of the old squares reached by a narrow archway from High Street. He had only two buses at any one time, both open, with folding canvas hoods. One was ES 6606, which he owned in 1925; another was a Chevrolet, SH 3429, which he bought from Whillis when they gave up. As a very small boy, I can just remember Redfearn's tours to Ford and Etal, etc., and I always wanted to go on them, but never did. To me the buses looked ancient but always well polished. Joe White was Redfearn's usual driver. Like S.E.Young of Spittal, Redfearn's business was basically a repair and sales garage. Young advertised Buick and Crossley; Redfearn sold Fiat, Bean and Overland.

10. BUSES ALONG THE COAST - TO SEAHOUSES AND BEYOND

Credit for the earliest start has been given already to S.E.CUTHBERTSON, Castle Garage, Seahouses, who had, from 1899, a horse bus working between Bamburgh and Seahouses to a timetable to connect with trains.

This was an interesting start. The North Sunderland Railway was a small private company. They had ideas of extending the railway as far as Monks House, half way from Seahouses to Bamburgh, ideas which did not come to fruition, so the horse bus connection was a cheap solution. By about 1904, two of the large railway companies, the Great Western and the North Eastern, saw the potential offered by motorbuses. They were the means of serving small towns which could not be served economically by new railway lines, or whose stations had to be built remote from the town because of opposition from the landowners.

Despite the reputation of the North Sunderland Railway as being 'the Flying Kipper', it was not always deserved - it was ahead of its time in this respect. The horse bus service was replaced or augmented by motor wagonettes, one in 1905, a second in 1907. Apart from the registration numbers, X 482 & X 958, nothing is known about those vehicles, or their fate. It is unlikely they survived into the 1914-18 War period.

About 1920, Cuthbertson bought a charabanc in addition to motor lorries. It was used only on the outings popular at the time - afternoon tours, football matches, etc. An older Seahouses resident told me, 'it was a funny looking bus, everybody came out to see it!'

Cuthbertson's Castle Garage at Seahouses, built partly of wood, was seriously damaged by fire in the late 1920s. Like many other early bus garages, the wooden building would have become impregnated with petrol and oil spillages. What remained of the garage was taken over by BOLTON BROS., of Embleton, becoming their Seahouses Garage until they sold out to United in 1936. But more of Boltons later.

Next to follow Cuthbertson in chronological order, I think, would be GEORGE PATTERSON & SONS, Beadnell. They commenced in 1921. What they actually did in the 1920s I have not been able to establish - it was probably outings with a charabanc. They did come to operate school contract buses and established bus services much later in the period. They continue to operate after nearly eighty years, now under the name 'Travelsure', and are the oldest established bus operators in Berwick Borough.

Coming now to regular timetabled services along the coast, HARRY BROOK, trading as AMBLE & DISTRICT, started in 1922 with a 39-seater charabanc and a 32-seater bus in April and June 1922 respectively. He did not run for long and the name 'Amble & District' passed to ROBERT KNOX, of Amble, late in 1922 or early 1923. It is unlikely that Harry Brook ever operated north of Alnwick, more probably he worked between Amble and Radcliffe.

Having disposed of the Amble business, Harry Brook went on to set up Brook and Amos, Galashiels, of which much more in a later chapter.

By the mid 1920s, KNOX was running a bus service from Alnwick to Berwick via Embleton, Seahouses, Bamburgh and Belford.

Mr.Hinson Stevenson, of North Sunderland, told me that, as a child, he lived at Brunton. The family had relatives at Haggerston whom they visited using Knox's bus. 'I remember it well', Hinson said, 'I was always sick!' The bus was a 14 seater, probably a Chevrolet. Hinson moved from Brunton in 1926. Another resident, living at Swinhoe as a child, used the bus to go to school at Beadnell when the weather was bad. 'It cost a ha'penny to travel, Jack Wake was the usual driver, but Tom Tully drove it on Jack's day off, and it was always late. Jack went to work for Boltons as a mechanic.'

On 22nd March 1928, J.Knox, of Amble, was fined £2.00 at Berwick Court for overloading. His 14-seater bus carried 27 adults and 2 children. The Chairman said it was becoming a serious matter. However, Knox was not alone in overloading.

Robert Knox operated in the Amble area, selling out his bus services in 1929 to LONGSTAFF, themselves one of the very early operators in Northumberland, and who still run today. Longstaff worked the main Warkworth-Amble-Morpeth -Newcastle service, selling that part of their business to United in 1936.

KNOX withdrew from the Alnwick-Berwick service around 1929 and WILLIAM RUTHERFORD, Northside, Craster, began to run. Whether he ran concurrently with, or subsequent to, Knox, I know not. Bus services into Berwick town had to have permission from Berwick Town Council before the 1930 Road Traffic Act came into force on 1st January 1931. The earliest reference to Rutherford in Berwick Council Minutes is on 21st January 1930 when he was authorised to operate an unspecified service until September 1930. He was, however, running a Craster-Newcastle service in the summer of 1927.

His timetable for summer 1932 advertises 'Rutherford's Coastal Coaches' offering a very good service between Alnwick and Berwick via Bamburgh with 'all buses arriving in Alnwick meeting connections for Alnmouth, Amble, Ashington, Morpeth, Wooler, Whitley Bay, and Newcastle.' This was the only service for which he had a licence.

Despite the good publicity, Rutherford was negotiating the sale of his business to United with agreement in October 1932, for £3250.

Rutherford owned eight buses, a mixed fleet of Chevrolet, Guy, Gilford and Star, of which, the oldest, the Chevrolet, NL 9770, dated from late 1925. He also ran taxis connecting with trains at Alnmouth. His staff included Norman Sanderson, George Swan, Jack Hadden, - Davidson and Nora Bell.

When William Rutherford came to the area, I am told he arrived at Little Mill by train, getting a bus to Craster run by ADAM ARCHBOLD, Ocean Garage, Craster. Strictly speaking, this is outside the scope of this book, but 'Little Adam' was one of Craster's characters.

As well as running a bus between Craster and Little Mill Station, Adam was Harbourmaster at Craster. I am told he had a bus about 1919. Certainly he had a 14 seater Ford bus, TY 53, new in 1925, and withdrawn in 1928 when he ceased trading. He called it 'Ocean Maid'.

Stories about Adam abound. Although he had a house in the village, he slept in the Harbourmaster's house when he thought it necessary. Another story is about his bus, I hope I have the story right!

A submarine had come ashore and been wrecked at Howick. Adam had obtained some brass work from it, which he hid under the seats in his bus. The local police had their suspicions but could not find the brass. Unfortunately for Adam, the bus was a bad starter and had to be push-started. This day he was unwise enough to ask the local constabulary to help him push it. They thought the bus was extremely heavy for its size, looked a little further, and found the missing brass.

BOLTON BROS., Embleton.

The brothers were Jack and Tommy. The family had had horses and traps which they hired out. Jack, a shoemaker, bought a 14 seater Maxwell charabanc, NL 6242, in 1923. He used this to run a daily service to Newcastle. He was lucky to be granted permission to park his bus, and to pick up passengers in the Haymarket there, one of the first to do so. Tommy joined the business, as did a sister, Dorothy.

The little Maxwell charabanc must have been inadequate as it was sold and replaced by a W & G Ducros 26 seater, TY 1738, in 1926 and another, TY 3446, in 1927, the latter a 32 seater. Bolton's, with their dark blue and cream livery, bought 'good' buses by the standards of the day.

From 1928 there were Leyland TS1 and TS2 Tigers, Leyland PLSC3 Lions, and Daimler CF6s. The last purchase was yet another W & G in 1931.

In many respects, Bolton Bros. were in a class of their own. Without turning this into a catalogue of technical details, a bit about the buses is worthwhile.

During the 1920s, makers of buses proliferated, with about sixty firms producing them. Originally, Leyland made steam lawn mowers, moving on to steam vehicles in 1896. In the early 1900s they began to develop their own petrol engines and had vehicles of their own design moving by 1907. The 1914-18 War saw them produce more than 6000 vehicles for the Royal Flying Corps, the forerunner of the RAF. After 1918 Leyland bought back from the Forces about half of those vehicles, basically lorries, which they reconditioned over some years. These were the vehicles favoured by the ex-servicemen who wanted to have convertible lorry/buses.

Leyland had developed on a scale unmatched by all except a small number of the sixty or so makers and, in time, they began to build bus bodies as well.

I mentioned earlier two types of theirs, the 'Lions' and the 'Tigers', which Boltons bought. The 'Lions' were the PLSC3 model introduced in 1926. Looking at old photos, they look really old-fashioned, but it was one of the most famous buses to be built. They were also reliable and survived well. Bolton's two 'Lions', TY 4792, and TY 5844, new in 1928 and 1929 respectively, went over to United. These buses were 26' long and 7'4" wide. Both 'Lions' and 'Tigers' had petrol engines. Diesel engines were just being developed and did not come into wide use until 1932/33.

Whilst the 'Lions' had sold well, Leyland sought a bolder design and introduced the 'Tiger' range, the prototype chassis appearing in 1927. The initial 'Tiger' was the model TS1. At 27'6" long, it was the maximum permitted length, giving about 32 seats. In 1928, the TS2 model was introduced, basically the same, but only 26' long.

At the time of their development the maximum permitted speed was still only 12 mph, but whether or not honoured is debatable. Since earlier buses were not designed for high speeds they could achieve 30 mph, or more, only at the expense of rough running. The TS models were an exception. They could still run smoothly at 30 mph, Leyland claiming they had a maximum speed, laden, of 52 mph. The extra power they generated made gear changing less frequent so less stress for the driver and more comfort for the passenger. These were crash gearboxes, unknown to most drivers today. They had no synchromesh, and you had to find the right level of engine revs. before the gear could be engaged, either up or down.

Boltons had two TS1s and one TS2, new between 1928 and 1930. They were taken over by United in 1936 and were not withdrawn until 1950, even after which, two of them went to work for building contractors. Given that Bolton's first bus, the little Maxwell of 1923, lasted two years, these lasted twenty-two years or more, so the comparison is obvious.

Boltons bought four Daimler CF6s, all second hand, from Scotland. Daimler, like Leyland, is one of the earliest names in the industry, building cars before 1900. Except during the 1914-18 War, they did not build lorries. Their first bus appeared in 1908, with many more built before 1914. Their history after 1918 is complicated by involvement with the AEC Company, forming Associated Daimler in 1926. United bought their buses, the 'ADCs'. Daimler returned to independence in 1928, developing the CF6 type, a 6-cylinder petrol-engined model. The company had pioneered pneumatic tyres for charabancs and further developments after the CF6 type included the use of the pre-selector gearbox. One of Bolton's Daimlers, VC 174, had been a demonstrator. Like the Tigers, their CF6 types passed to United, two of them working until 1950.

But to return to Bolton's services. Their basic service, as begun in 1923, was that between Bamburgh and Newcastle via Beadnell and Alnwick, although duplicate buses often avoided Alnwick to save time for through passengers. They had other operation on a limited scale between Alnwick, Chathill and Seahouses, and they carried schoolchildren to the Duke's School, Alnwick.

From an operating viewpoint, the Newcastle-Bamburgh service was difficult. In winter, buses were not busy. In summer, and particularly at weekends, buses were extremely busy. They

Leyland Lion TY5844 of Bolton Bros stands outside their Embleton garage. It passed to United in 1936 as fleet number LL25. The crew have not been identified. *(R.C.Davis)*

What the well-dressed youth wore. Helping at the petrol pumps at Boltons. *(R.C.Davis)*

could leave Newcastle with standing loads, with duplicates, and with buses hired from Main and other small firms. Thus Bolton had to have more vehicles than would have been the case had he had an even traffic movement - so costs were inflated.

Their original garage was at Embleton. When Cuthbertson's garage at Seahouses had fire damage, the 'solid' part remaining was taken over by Bolton as a second garage. As well as that, they kept a bus and a crew at Newcastle to work the first journey from there in the morning and bring the last in at night.

A couple of local residents told me about Boltons. Gordon Pitt, who, sadly, died before completion of the book, had worked for them. He recalled their Leylands, one of which had a sunroof. He remembered the W & G Ducros, nicknamed 'the wobbly ganner'. He said that Jack did a lot of the driving. 'It was extremely busy during the summer peak - Jack used to stand in the Haymarket, wearing his big watch chain, and push the passengers in - it was always standing loads', said Gordon. 'Boltons had a 5/- return to Newcastle and football matches there were well patronised'. He recalled, too, some of the other staff, including J.Hamilton, G.Henderson, J.Wake, D.Veitch, B.Dawson, R.Hope, P.Ogle, and N.Humble.

As a boy, Norman McKay lived next door to their Seahouses Garage. He was too young to drive buses but did puncture repairs, etc., a bit of conducting and helped with the hiring of buses for football matches. Tommy Bolton, I'm told, was more at the garage, and 'did the organisation.' 'He had two voices- an everyday one and a posh one for answering the phone.'

Another snippet from them concerned the Seahouses lifeboat. Having been out, it had to be pulled in manually. If the lifeboat needed assistance a bus was brought from Bolton's garage and a line attached to it. The bus then reversed and, with manual help, towed the lifeboat in. It could happen even when the bus was in service to or from Newcastle and happened to be passing Seahouses. Passengers had to leave the bus and wait until it had towed the lifeboat.

As well as good buses, Bolton had good publicity. They published their own little book, 'Northumbria's Riviera', every year. It carried timetables for their bus services, lists of their tours, something about the places and their history - and advertising. United saw fit to continue it when they took over.

I was intrigued by one of the adverts. 'Don't spend your holiday shopping. Leave your order the night previous and it will be at your house before 9 o'clock the next morning. Ring up Seahouses 265, and I will deliver within half an hour. Send me a postcard stating date of arrival, and I will arrange to deliver at any time to suit your convenience. It was Henry Alder, the butcher, who offered that.

With its summer peaks and winter troughs in passenger traffic, Jack and Tommy Bolton could not afford to replace the bus fleet. They, too, went the way of others, and on 28th May 1936, their dark blue and cream buses passed to United. So went one of the most interesting bus companies in Northumberland.

United kept Service 60, Alnwick-Chathill-Seahouses. The Newcastle-Bamburgh service was routed via Warkworth and Alnmouth, and not Alnwick, becoming Service 29, and running through to Berwick. Service 51 was the Alnwick-Craster-Bamburgh service, it running also through to Belford and, sometimes Berwick. Boltons kept their motor garage at Embleton. United needed to keep a bus in the Seahouses area. In May 1937 they took a three-year lease on the former Presbyterian Church in North Street, North Sunderland. The premises were vacated on 12th August 1940 due to 'petrol restrictions and the commandeering of buses.' United did return buses to Seahouses out-station in due course; today they just park in the car park.

The only bus operator found in Belford was JAMES FORD, originally from Plantation, but later at West Street, Belford. It seems he had a convertible lorry/bus between 1923 and 1925.

HOLY ISLAND always had its own transport facilities, taxis, especially to suit visitors staying on the Island. I only ever saw elderly taxis - suffering the effects of the salt water - and costing 10/- for the trip. I never used them. Some Islanders had licences to operate across to Beal Station to connect with trains under the 1930 legislation but none had any in force after 1931. They were: -

ROBERT BELL, Post Office, Holy Island.
S.J.LUKE, Iron Rails Hotel, Holy Island.
G.W and R.A.WILSON, Manor House, Holy Island

Model T Fords were used as Island taxis. Robinson's Garage at Lowick maintained them and were the last people to hold a stock of spares for them.

Buses would not come on to the Island until the causeway opened; service buses not until the bridge over the Low was completed in the 1970s.

11. BUSES COME TO WOOLER AND GLENDALE

Wooler and Glendale got their railway in 1887, so there was little need for buses in early years. Cornhill had its station in 1849. The earliest requirement was for buses for outings when these began to be popular about 1920.

Rather than deal with individual operators in alphabetical or datal order, this chapter is arranged on an area basis.

CORNHILL AREA.

To avoid repetition, this deals only with the very localised services around Cornhill. Bus services on the A 697 are described below, and those between Kelso and Berwick appear in a later chapter on the SMT.

JOHN CONQUER, Pallinsburn, who was a haulage contractor before the 1914 War, had a bus in 1921, which he used for outings. Nothing is known about it.

HENRY PATTERSON, Branxton, had a charabanc from about 1926. This was used on outings but also made regular trips to Berwick and possibly elsewhere. It survived until his death about 1930. Mr.Patterson also hired cars.

EARLY OPERATORS IN WOOLER

JAMES RENTON AND SON, Pethhead, Wooler, was the first known. He was in business with a charabanc in 1920 for outings. Later he began a competitive service from Wooler to Newcastle which is explained below. He owned one or two buses. His business survived until 1934, having obtained licences for his Newcastle-Coldstream service and for excursions and tours from Wooler.

E.SCOTT, High Street, Wooler was another early comer, starting in 1921. He had only one bus, again used for outings, and he traded until 1926.

J.W.YOUNG, West House, Norham was the first with a regular service into Wooler, that from Berwick which he began in 1923/24. His service continued until March 1934 when he sold out to United. More about him in the Berwick chapter.

WILLIAM WILSON PILE, Market Place, Wooler was yet another early trader, with one bus and outings from 1921. He pioneered the Wooler-Newcastle service and his operation is outlined in the next section.

JOHN STENHOUSE, Town Yetholm ran into Wooler from Kirknewton and Yetholm. He ran services from Yetholm to Berwick and to Kelso; selling out in 1934, part to United, part to SMT.

12. WOOLER TO NEWCASTLE & EDINBURGH

W.W.PILE

Several companies served these routes, the pioneer being W.W.PILE, whose garage was at 18, Station Road, Wooler. He began a daily return service from Wooler to Newcastle at Easter 1926. For this he bought a new bus, a W & G Ducros 26 seater, TY 465. The service was immediately successful and was soon increased to twice daily. The first driver on the route was Tommy Nesham soon joined by Arthur MacLean. Both worked a lifetime on the local buses, Tommy, a driver with United at Wooler; Arthur, who became Depot Foreman at United's Wooler Depot.

Pile bought more new buses, another W & G, a 28 seater, in 1927, and a small Studebaker in 1928. That year, 1928, he extended his Newcastle-Wooler service through to Edinburgh via Coldstream and Kelso. In addition to private hire, he ran an extended tour of Scotland in 1928. Competition rife from other operators, Pile sold out to United in November 1928.

JAMES RENTON AND SON

An early starter in the business, he noted Pile's success on the Newcastle route. He started on it in 1927, advertising a 'Daily Pullman-Saloon Service', for which he had bought a Reo Pullman 26 seater, TY 3238. He got licences for a Newcastle-Coldstream service and for excursions and tours from Wooler in 1930, trading until 1934, when he gave up the business.

COUNTY MOTOR SERVICES LTD, Stakeford

Gordon Bros. started County Motors in 1924 with earliest services from Newcastle to Ashington and to Whitley Bay. In September 1927 they began a new venture, a Newcastle - Wooler - Kelso - Edinburgh - Glasgow service.

They offered a daily trip from Newcastle to Glasgow, twice daily to Edinburgh, taking five hours, and with extra journeys, Newcastle Kelso, and Wooler-Edinburgh. This gave excellent new opportunities. Local fares were available and you could have a day out from Wooler to Edinburgh for 10/9d (54p) return. Their publicity showed 'County Bus Stations' at Haymarket, Newcastle and Chambers Street, Edinburgh. They had agents, E.Scott at Wooler, and Crombie at Coldstream. So, at September 1927, there are three operators running between Newcastle and Wooler.

There was also competition on the north side. John Turnbull, of Kelso, ran from there to Edinburgh while SMT were developing their Edinburgh-Jedburgh service.

In November 1929 County Motors began a new overnight limited stop service from Glasgow to London, calling at Edinburgh, Coldstream (9.0pm), Wooler (9.45pm), Newcastle and Doncaster, arriving London at 10.0am. With comfortable coaches it was another local transport revolution. The only disadvantage was that, on the northbound journey, passengers for Wooler, etc., had to change into the stopping bus at Newcastle.

They kept one bus and two crews at Coldstream; their drivers were Tommy Purvis and Harry Hardy, two more United Wooler stalwarts.

County obtained licences for these services in 1930 and they ran until sold to United and SMT by an agreement dated 2nd January 1933. Five buses went to SMT. The date of take over is later, probably 23rd April. County did not sell out completely in 1933. They continued in Ashington until finally selling to United in 1937.

THOMAS ALLEN AND SONS, BLYTH

Allens were one of the first operators in Northumberland. They were running horse drawn wagonettes between Blyth and Bebside before the arrival of buses. Having run buses in south east Northumberland for years, they were late in the day in coming to Wooler. Early in 1931 they were granted a licence for a daily service from Newcastle to Aberdeen, following the same route as County to Edinburgh, then via Stirling, Perth, Dundee and Montrose, taking twelve hours. Despite the lengthy journey there were many local fares, in this case a 6/-d (30p)

County Motors bought this Leyland Tiger TS1, TY5245, in 1929 to work the Newcastle - Wooler - Edinburgh - Glasgow service. It awaits departure from Haymarket, Newcastle. It did not pass to United until 1937, becoming fleet number LT98 before being sold later that year. Note the Edinburgh licence on the bus. *(R.Grieves)*

Thomas Allen bought this Leyland Tiger TS1, TY8670, in July 1931. It is all dressed up for the long run from Newcastle to Aberdeen via Wooler and Kelso. It was sold to United, becoming AT254, later LT51. *(Leyland Motors)*

return between Wooler and Newcastle. Allen sold out to United in 1934, the latter not taking over the licence for the Aberdeen service, which was discontinued.

UNITED AUTOMOBILE SERVICES LTD

Having acquired W.W.Pile by agreement of November 1928, United came to Wooler. Dates of purchase agreements do not usually co-incide with operational dates. Thus United's actual arrival in Wooler would be summer 1929. Their timetable dated 5th June 1929 shows their Service 21, Newcastle-Wooler-Coldstream three times daily with an extra Wooler trip on Saturdays, 'as previously operated by W.W.Pile's buses.' In addition, a footnote says that 'the return halves of United tickets between Newcastle and Longframlington are valid on the buses of Pile, John Lee & Son, or Wright's Saloon Service, or vice versa.' Lee and Wright, both of Rothbury, were bought by United at the same time as Pile. With this timetable, a bus starts in service at Coldstream, while the extra Saturday service from Wooler to Newcastle shows positioning journeys between Berwick and Wooler. Berwick staff must have run these trips at some time. At Coldstream, connections are shown to and from Kelso and Edinburgh by SMT.

Having come to Wooler in 1929, United had seen Pile go; they would see County go, and then Renton give up. Across the Border, Turnbull of Kelso went, leaving the SMT clear and the way forward for United and SMT to have their joint Services 15/510, Newcastle-Wooler-Edinburgh.

Exactly how and where United set up in Wooler is not clear. They paid rent to W.W.Pile in 1930-31, so presumably they rented his garage having taken over his service. At the same period they were renting part of premises in Station Road, Wooler, now South Road, from Glendale Garage. The whole of that garage was rented from December 1935 and bought in 1949.

13. WOOLER-GLANTON-ALNWICK

Since a different batch of private operators set up this route, their history is taken together. They were: -

> THOMAS R.GRAY, Green Batt Garage, Alnwick;

> JOHN CAIRNS, Warkworth, later Glanton;
> G.HILTON & W.COXON, Learchild, Whittingham; and
> J.J.MORDUE, Edlingham.

This route, going via Lemmington Bank, Whittingham, Glanton and the A 697, generated much competition and acrimony. GRAY, with a 14 seater Reo, NL 9718, in June 1925, would be the first to run; CAIRNS began in September 1926; MORDUE started about 1927 and HILTON had a bus in 1928.

Some of the history of the route was given in 1970 when Mr.John Cairns gave a talk to the now defunct Aln & Breamish Local History Society.

Mr.Cairns' father came on to this route in September 1926 with a 14 seater Chevrolet, making three return trips daily. Early in 1927, he increased his service. The extra trips and heavy loads put a strain on the bus on Lemmington Bank. Frequent overheating occurred so that passengers left the bus and walked further up the hill, being picked up when the bus cooled down and got on its way. He was never able to overcome the problem with the Chevrolet so next he bought a more powerful 20 seater International. This one did not have overheating problems, but it had trouble on Lemmington Bank due to the gravity-fed petrol supply. On the steepest part of the Bank the level of petrol in the tank could be lower than that in the carburettor, cutting off the fuel supply. Mr.Cairns said that, to begin with, they criss-crossed the bus up the hill - which worked - until he solved the problem by fitting an autovac.

These were not the only troubles. Punctures were prevalent for which drivers carried a repair outfit and a foot pump. They didn't bother to fit the spare. Brakes had to be adjusted after most journeys over Lemmington Bank; wheel nuts had to be tightened at the risk of losing a wheel.

Mr.Cairns also spoke about springs. A blacksmith in the old Star Yard in Alnwick was adept at making and setting them. What comes over in his talk and with others with whom I have spoken is that they were 'little men' and not big companies. They had to learn by their mistakes as they went - there was not a pool of experienced mechanics waiting to do their repairs, and certainly few factory-trained people His point contradicts what I wrote earlier in the

Wooler High Street in 1950. A rebodied AEC waits to depart for Newcastle.

Y 4633 was one of two Albion PFB26 models bought by T.R.Gray, Alnwick in 1928. Note the canvas hood. It passed to United in 1931 as fleet number CM83, working from Wooler. It was sold to W.Alexander & Sons, Falkirk and then to Robertson, Lockerbie. *(R.Grieves)*

book that the 1914-18 War left many ex-servicemen with mechanical experience. To a great extent it did, but in the ensuing years up to the mid and late 1920s there were, literally, dozens of manufacturers building buses. Busmen had to learn how to deal with the idiosyncrasies of the various makes - so, indeed you had to learn by your mistakes.

In September 1927 they bought another new bus, this time a 6-cyl. Reo, to do the school contract from Wooler to Alnwick. Shortly after that, a Saturday service was introduced between Alnwick, Whittingham, Callaly and Netherton. Cairns' plan to extend the service from Netherton to Rothbury, giving a through service from Alnwick was thwarted when Lee of Rothbury extended his Newcastle - Thropton service to Netherton.

Further competition came in 1927 when J.J.MORDUE began to run. In 1928, more competition, this time from HILTON & COXON.

We know that T.R.Gray had at least five buses, including two Albions and two Reos, which were bought by United when Gray sold out to them in late 1931.

George Hilton had a 20 seater Thornycroft that he sold to United with his business in late 1932. After 1930 he ran only between Alnwick and Glanton. He also had a workmens' service between Alnwick and Shilbottle. George was another stalwart who spent the rest of his working life with United, retiring from Wooler depot. The agreement by United to buy his business was different in detail from others in that 'it did not preclude William Coxon from operating a Workmens' Service once daily in each direction between Alnwick and Shilbottle or preclude George Hilton from being employed by the purchasers in any capacity'.

Mr. Cairns' talk tells about an unnamed operator (Mordue?) who set up in opposition with a lorry/bus they named 'The Box'. It was used as a lorry during the week to carry coal; at weekends it had a box-shaped body fitted to carry passengers.

He goes on to tell that the acrimony was eventually overcome and a joint timetable agreed, giving a two-hourly service between Glanton and Alnwick on Mondays to Fridays and hourly on Saturdays, some journeys going on to Wooler. That had to happen as none of the

operators was making a living due to the cut-throat competition. There was still a big demand for buses for private parties on outings, and to football matches, etc.

Approaching 1931, the prospect of the Road Traffic Act and, of the seemingly predatory activities of the United, no doubt raised concern in all their minds. Cairns lost his best vehicle in a fire. A replacement of that was not financially viable so he pulled out of the operation. Mordue too, gave up, leaving Gray and Hilton to obtain licences and soldier on for a time. When Gray finally sold out in late 1931, United had the Alnwick-Wooler service to themselves - Service 21.

WOOLER-CHATTON-ALNWICK.

In January 1926, JAMES ALLAN, Post Office Chatton, started this route with a 14 seater Graham Dodge, TY 462. In 1928 he was joined by Alex. Henderson to form ALLAN & HENDERSON, Chatton.

By the standards of the day they had a charmed life. They were the sole operators through Chatton, Chillingham and Eglingham even if they had competition for through passengers from the Glanton operators. Two more new buses were bought in 1928, small Dodges, SL 2413 and TY 4302, then in 1930 a 20 seater Commer, TY 7365. They continued in business with the licence needed for the route from 1931

By 1934 the small operators were literally 'going down like ninepins' to the United. Allan & Henderson must have seen themselves out on a limb. They sold their business, including three buses, to United on 17th March 1934 for £2600 As usual the vendors were precluded from operating or having any financial interest in any bus service in Northumberland or Durham for five years. The actual date of take over was 1st June 1934, the route becoming Service 70.

They did return to the bus business in 1960 running two small buses until 1972.

John Young of Norham had served Chatton on Saturdays only for a period in the early 1930s in connection with his Berwick-Wooler service United did not continue that having bought Young's business in 1934 but they did, from February 1938, extend a couple of Lowick duplicates to provide a Saturday service, Service 68, between Berwick and Chatton.

14. THE RISE OF UNITED

United Automobile Services Ltd. did not come to Berwick until 1928 so they were by no means one of the earliest operators in the Borough. They were a very old established bus company with an interesting history. That history is well documented and anyone wishing to read about it should seek a copy of Nigel Watson's book, 'United - a short history of United Automobile Services Ltd. 1912 - 1987' or a much more comprehensive two-volume hardback history of United to be published in 2001 and 2002 by Venture Publications. There is also a 'Fleet History of United', published by the PSV Circle. Nevertheless a bit of United's history is not amiss here.

The Company was formed early in 1912 operating buses between Lowestoft and Southwold in competition with the Railway Company's buses. In the autumn of 1912, they began to run buses in Bishop Auckland.

While United started in a small way with two second hand Halley charabancs, they were also a registered company with E.B.Hutchinson as Managing Director and a London office. Their bus services in East Anglia and County Durham were expanded quickly.

Nigel Watson has an interesting quote from United's rulebook of the time: - 'conductors are expected to learn to drive, but this must be done when there are few passengers in the car'. United always used the term 'car' for their buses.

The outbreak of War in 1914 created immediate problems for United. Their fleet of thirty-five buses was split with seventeen in South Durham and eighteen in the Lowestoft/Yarmouth area. Within a few days all eighteen from Lowestoft had been commandeered by the War Office. Their chassis went for conversion to Army lorries; their bodies were left in store for the duration of the War. They got almost no compensation. Buses being a new industry, all staff were of military age and all fit men went into the Army. E.B.Hutchinson reported that 'for drivers we got the halt, the lame, the young, the old, and we even tried girls (as bus drivers) who, in the prevailing conditions, were not a success.' 'Petrol supplies were limited so the single-deck buses were run on gas carried in large bags on the roof. The gas supply had to be replenished after twelve miles of running. On one occasion a boy burst a gas bag with an air gun and stopped the bus.'

When the War ended in 1918 they had to start over again using converted Army lorries or whatever they could press into service. They did expand from 1919, both by new services and by buying out small operators in East Anglia and the North East. Garages were built at Blyth and Ashington by 1923. These were the years of intensive competition. Nigel Watson quotes a comment by United's Chairman in 1923, '...many men have been tempted, seeing the success of United, to buy a bus and run it on their own, they themselves or a family member being both driver and conductor. We run to timetable, they are free to run as they please, and they make a practice of starting off on a particular route five minutes before our buses start and pick up passengers as they go along before us.' He continued, referring to unfair competition, '...we cannot overcome it all but, hair-by-hair, we are pulling out the horse's tail.' Little did he know how history would come very near to repeating itself sixty years later.

United's extensions were not merely in the North East. They extended into Norfolk, Lincolnshire, Derbyshire, Yorkshire and Teesside. In 1920 they opened a factory in Lowestoft to refurbish wartime chassis and build bus bodies. This body building unit grew large enough to be formed into Eastern Coachworks Ltd. in 1936, continuing in business until 1987.

From its original office in London in 1912 United moved to Lowestoft in 1913 then to York in 1926. With an operating area from Suffolk to Northumberland United was becoming unwieldy. It was also viewed with alarm by the railway companies who saw this vast operating territory as a threat to themselves. Roles were now reversed. The railways obtained new powers to buy major interests in road passenger transport, while the 'big boys' of the bus industry, Tilling and British Automobile Traction, together provided a threat to United's independence. After wrangling at Board level, United eventually passed to the joint control of the LNE Railway and Tilling/BAT in 1929. Thus E.B.Hutchinson as a dissenting Director, also departed, having built up United from the two charabancs to 660 buses. This vast undertaking was broken up into more manageable constituent

TY 4633, a Graham-Dodge 14-seater, was Allan & Henderson's first bus, bought in 1926. Jimmy Allan is standing at the front and the photograph was taken just round the corner from the Chatton garage.

Allan & Henderson's last purchase was a 1930 Commer, TY 7365. This vehicle passed to United when Allan & Henderson sold out. The roof rack suggests that farm produce was carried.

companies - Eastern Counties, East Midland Motor Services, Lincolnshire Road Car Co., etc., leaving the 'rump' United running in Northumberland, Durham and North Yorkshire, and moving its Head Office from York to Darlington.

By now it had reached Berwick. That makes the next chapter.

15. UNITED AUTOMOBILE SERVICES LTD - HOW THEY CAME TO BERWICK

In the previous chapter I set out a thumbnail history of United. The Company had come to County Durham and south Northumberland by 1920. Being heavily populated it was likely to be profitable bus territory. There were many small operators and aggressive competition. United came to Berwick in 1928 as a result of circumstances rather than potential profitability so it is necessary to explain what had taken place on the A1 road.

F.W.Jermy of Felton had served the section between Newcastle and Alnwick efficiently since 1924.

Between Alnwick and Berwick there was no bus service. The low permitted speed for buses - 12 mph - in force until the late 1920s ensured that they could not have competed with the rail service. The twenty nine miles by road would have needed more than two hours to be legal and, even allowing for a change of trains at Alnmouth, the train had the advantage. Moreover trains gave a reasonable local service with stations at Scremerston, Goswick, Beal, Belford, Lucker, Newham, Chathill, etc.

That would all change on 8th August 1927 when AMOS, PROUD & CO., of Choppington, who had been running between Ashington and Newcastle, started to run from Newcastle to Edinburgh via Alnwick, Berwick and Dunbar. They used 'big' buses, 31/32 seaters, scheduled at 20 mph. They based several buses at Berwick, transferring staff from Choppington to crew them and one at Dunbar, the crew there being R.Buglass and L.Wilson.

A month later COUNTY MOTOR SERVICES, from Stakeford, began a similar service from Newcastle to Glasgow via Wooler, Kelso and Edinburgh.

At that time SMT ran Edinburgh-Dunbar and Edinburgh-Kelso. These two new operators

posed a threat. SMT extended their Dunbar service to Berwick in June 1928, keeping a bus and crew at Berwick.

Meantime United were active and, following the opening of the Royal Tweed Bridge in May 1928, they recruited at, or transferred drivers and conductors to work at Berwick. In the summer of 1928 SMT and United jointly began an hourly service between Newcastle, Berwick and Edinburgh in competition with Amos, Proud. The United timetable for July 1928 shows Service 22 as a joint through service. In practice, for a few months, passengers could book through but they had to change buses at Berwick. United ran Berwick-Newcastle; SMT ran Berwick-Edinburgh, which now needed two buses. SMT had to bring crews from Edinburgh to run the two buses now garaged at Berwick; drivers R.Grant, E.Gray and J.Swordy; conductors J.Harkness, S.Robertson and T.Mar. The reason for this will be explained in a moment. Meanwhile, F.W.Jermy, who had run the Newcastle-Alnwick service, was faced with serious competition from Amos, Proud and United.

The threat posed by Amos, Proud and County Motors was not merely to bus operators. It threatened the railways themselves who, until then, had had a monopoly of long distance passengers. The very existence of this growing giant, United, was also a threat.

Since early 1900s the railways had been operating a few bus services themselves but they wanted to test the legality. Legislation in 1928 empowered them to do so, but only under strict conditions. For example, a railway owned bus route could operate only with the consent of the Minister of Transport and be withdrawn after notice in the 'London Gazette'. Thus the railways decided to buy into bus companies in preference to starting up themselves under the impossible conditions they had to meet.

The London & North Eastern Railway bought a controlling interest in Amos, Proud early in 1928, United taking over the bus operation for the LNER later that year. That removed the competition on the Newcastle-Berwick-Edinburgh service between Amos, Proud and United and the two groups of staff at Berwick came under one management.

By this time 'giants' were rising in the bus industry - the Tilling Group and British

VF 4180 was United's Leyland Tiger B271, new in November 1928. It was renumbered AT38 in 1930. It had been ordered by Pioneer Bus Service, Whitby and delivered to United when Pioneer sold out. This photo is posed on Berwick's Quayside when the bus was on delivery to United's Berwick depot. The driver is Tommy Miller, ex-Amos, Proud. The civilian is Mr. Bunn, the Area Engineer. The vehicle was not likely to have departed for Glasgow, despite the blind.

Lamp standards in the middle of the street; pedestrians crossing Golden Square junction; hardly any cars; lots of passengers. Berwick High Street in 1930 or earlier. The buses visible belong to John Young, Norham. They include Albion PB24 NL 7137, Lancia NL9374, with Young's Vulcan at the rear. The policeman on point duty has been replaced by a roundabout! *(Both: R.Grieves)*

Automobile Traction. 'United' was independent and a target for both giants as well as the LNE Railway. Following dissension in the Board and the departure of the founder of United, E.B.Hutchinson, the shareholders accepted an offer whereby the LNER and the now-amalgamated Tilling/BAT each took an equal stake in United.

Eighteen months later came the 1930 Road Traffic Act with licensing of bus services to reduce wasteful competition; with proper vehicle maintenance standards and the licensing of bus drivers and conductors centrally. Many small operators could not cope with the regulations and either sold out or gave up.

As already noted, the Newcastle-Berwick-Edinburgh route was, in 1928, running hourly jointly by United and SMT. In fact there was a complication. In order to run buses then permission had to be sought from the local Councils, some of whom were strict in granting licences, not only for buses, but also for individual employees. Gordon Wilson told me how he had to go to Edinburgh, taking references, before getting a licence to work into Edinburgh as a conductor. Berwick's United crews were granted licences by Edinburgh City Council. Amos, Proud and SMT had obtained licences for their buses to pick up and set down passengers in Edinburgh. United had not. Having got control of Amos, Proud was one thing - getting licences for their own buses was another. There was a novel solution. Four of the Leyland buses United had taken over from Amos, Proud

Left: VF 4178 or 4179, United AL28 or 29, a Leyland PLSC Lion, new in 1928. The bus was ordered by Amos, Proud but delivered to United. It stands inside the A&B Garage in Berwick on Good Friday 1935. Percy Tweddle, the mechanic, is on the left.; Watson Curry, 'the archetypal busman', on the right.

Right: VF 7603, United's AEC Reliance AK33, stands in Wooler c.1935. Jackie Oliver, ex-Spowart Bros, is the driver.

in November 1928 (TY 2423, 3066, 3677, 3678) were painted in SMT livery, but operated by United crews until Edinburgh licences were obtained for the buses. They were then transferred to the SMT in 1929.

So from early 1929 United were settled in Berwick, running mainly to Newcastle and Edinburgh with the odd journey between Wooler and Newcastle. That would remain so until 1932 when RUTHERFORD, of Craster, was bought. They had operated an Alnwick-Berwick service via Embleton, Seahouses, Bamburgh and Belford.

By agreements of November 1933 and, operationally in March 1934, three of the four private operators running in Berwick were bought - SPOWART, THOMPSON, and YOUNG. Those purchases brought in services to Spittal, Scremerston, Wooler, Norham, Ford and Crookham, leaving only a single private operator

running into Berwick from the south. STENHOUSE, of Yetholm sold out to United and SMT in an agreement of 22nd September 1934. Concurrently SMT was buying out and most of the independent bus services north of the Border had gone. How the SMT developed and the stories behind Spowart, Thompson, Young and Stenhouse appear in subsequent chapters.

But to return to AMOS, PROUD/UNITED.

I wrote earlier that Amos, Proud came to Berwick in August 1927. The name 'Amos' appears twice in local transport history; once in Amos, Proud, who came from Choppington, and in Brook & Amos, from Galashiels. As far as I know they are two different Amos families.

J.W.Proud started up in 1924, being joined in 1925 by H.Amos to form a limited company, Amos, Proud & Co. (1925) Ltd., running about thirty buses around Ashington.

Amos, Proud had been able to obtain licences

from Edinburgh City Council to allow them to run into the city and they recruited three drivers named Davidson, Fairbairn and McLachlan, and a conductress, Mrs.McLachlan, in Edinburgh where they were based. They transferred six of their existing staff from Choppington to Berwick - Tommy Miller, Ninian Kinross, Watson Curry, B.Scott, H.Rickleton and Tweddle, together with three buses - Leylands - in their dark green livery.

That was August 1927. United could not stand by and see that happen. They decided to launch a competitive service along the A1 until such time as Amos, Proud could be 'dealt with'. They transferred staff to, or recruited at Berwick. The drivers were Bill Cossar and Cyril Hooley; the conductors Gordon Wilson and G.Thompson. United had their service going by July 1928.

At first the United buses were garaged at Boston's Fish Yard in Sandstell Road, Spittal. Cyril Hooley was the driver-in-charge. He lived in Ravensdowne, Berwick, the front room of his house being the office accomodation. Berwick was then an out-station of Alnwick Depot where Mr.Knox was in charge. Boston's Yard was not used for long and buses were moved first to Main Street, Tweedmouth, where the Co-op Supermarket now stands, and then to the Alnwick & Berwick motor garage (the A & B) in Silver Street, Berwick. They remained there until the agreement was terminated on 20th October 1937, or maybe earlier, but certainly when the Bus Station opened. There is a tenancy agreement of early 1934 i.e. when Spowart, Thompson and Young were acquired. For a 14 seater bus United paid 7/6d (38p) per week; for one of thirty or more seats, 10/6d per week. For an office and storeroom the rent was 14/- per week. That agreement allowed eight buses to be garaged.

The Foreman at the A&B was Percy Tweddle, with his broad Northumbrian speech. The mechanic was Charlie Dunbar. He was welding a petrol tank without having made absolutely sure it was clear of fumes. The tank ended up in the rafters. I'm told that, having done it, he rang Mr.Jowett, the Area Engineer at Newcastle, and said, 'did you hear that bang?' 'no, what bang?' 'there's a petrol tank made a hole in the roof.' I never got the reply recorded!

I never knew Charlie Dunbar, he was there long before my time, but another story was told of him. He was working as an inspector and checking a bus. On the bus was a regular traveller known to everyone (and me later) as Sammy the Jew. He was a travelling draper, harmless, but a bit of a nuisance. Charlie boarded the bus to find Sammy with his boots off. He was not pleased with the ozone level and told Sammy to put his boots on. Sammy refused so Charlie picked up the boots and threw them off the moving bus!

There was no office at Berwick. However buses carried parcels - a lot of them - for which Parcels Agents were found. United had Aird and Mitchelson, both with shops in High Street. The latter, at no. 102, had a little shop on the corner, just above the 'Advertiser' office. Buses stopping there were creating a traffic hazard. From 1st June 1933, United used the SMT office at 88, High Street for all parcels, enquiries and bookings at a rent of £130 per year. That arrangement was short-lived as they rented two rooms (with the use of a common outhouse and lavatory) at 15, West Street from 1st December 1933. That is now the front section of Dalgleish's men's shop. The outhouse and toilet were up the yard at the side, which, in Berwick fashion, housed quite a number of tenants in single rooms, as well as Lewis' bakery. On the narrow West Street it was not in a very convenient situation but it survived until 1937, and at £26.00 per year plus rates, it was not bad. I was a small boy living opposite at the time. We had an 'apartment' up a yard, with every inconvenience, at a rent of £5.20 per year. But more about the West Street office later.

So, United and the former Amos, Proud staffs were together at the A&B Garage in Berwick, working to and from Newcastle and Edinburgh. That would continue until March 1934 when the three independents, Spowart, Thompson and Young were taken over.

But a bit more about United, and their early marketing policies. Post boxes were fitted to some buses with letters being accepted on certain journeys listed in the timetable. Bus crews had nothing to do with them, letters being taken off the bus by postmen. Another pre-war feature was that some buses had cigarette machines fixed to the bulkhead. You could come down to the bus stop, the bus would wait while you put your shilling into the machine and got a packet of 'Craven A' and a ha'penny change. Again, bus crews took no part other than waiting for you. The machines were stocked up at Newcastle.

Much earlier, and before United came to Berwick, they had a marketing scheme with Kodak to attract passengers from competitors. It was described in the staff magazine of the day. Kodak photographed various castles, churches, etc., in United's area, these being made into cards similar to the cigarette cards then popular. These were given to conductors to be issued to any passenger who bought a return ticket costing more than one shilling. They came in sets of twenty-five different views; anyone presenting a full set was given a Kodak camera free. It was said to be extremely difficult to collect a set unless you travelled widely on United. The conductors would not able to give them out willy-nilly. United used face value tickets so it was easy to tell how many of the appropriate values they had sold. The cards would have to be accounted for.

Starting with E.B.Hutchinson in 1912, United generated its characters. As Area Traffic Superintendent for Northumberland until about 1950 was Randolph Emmerson. He started with a 14-seater charabanc in 1921 in Throckley and, with his brother, built up a network in the Tyne Valley. With a service between Newcastle, Hexham and Carlisle he was another 'threat' to the LNE Railway. They eventually bought him out, the share capital being transferred to the United in 1930. The Emmerson brothers were thus debarred under the agreement from operating, or having a financial interest in bus services south of a line from North Berwick to Dumbarton, and north of a line from Lancaster to Scarborough. United took Randolph Emmerson, a down-to-earth Walbottle man, into the company to which he was an asset. His successor was Gibson French, one of two brothers who, with another partner, set up the Northallerton Omnibus Company in 1924. They had about twenty buses operating in North Yorkshire and the Dales. Financial difficulties forced their sale to United in June 1930, Gibson becoming Outside Traffic Assistant at Bedale depot. I transferred from Berwick to Newcastle District Office in August 1953 when he was there. A quiet, dour man, not in the best of health, I don't think I ever saw him smile. Northumberland Area, at that time, covered a triangle between Berwick, Newcastle and Carlisle. It had 375

buses in winter, increasing to 430 in the summer timetable. After Gibson French retired, Havelock Farrar, another long-standing and well-respected United man took over at Newcastle.

In the upper echelons the prominent figure after E.B.Hutchinson was Albert Thomas Evans. He was Company Secretary 1925-1934; Traffic Manager 1930-1934; General Manager 1934-1959. Stories about him are legion. When I left the RAF in 1949 I wrote to the 'General Manager' to see if there was a job available. He sent for me and I got a job at Berwick, Nancy Taylor having just left. In 1956 I moved from the Newcastle District Office to Darlington Head Office. The first instruction I received was, 'Albert's office is upstairs - don't try to pass him on the stairs. If you don't wait for him, he'll go back, and he doesn't like that.'

Albert had a dog. He was seen at Whitby Bus Station one Saturday with Mrs.Evans and the dog. Some time later, an identical dog was seen running around the Bus Station on its own. The Inspector's immediate thought was, 'Albert's dog is lost'. The dog was duly apprehended, had an 'On Company's Service' label attached to its collar and given to a conductor on Service 65 with instructions to hand it over at Middlesbrough to a Darlington bus. Half an hour later, Albert, Mrs.Evans - and the dog - were seen in the Bus Station. Panic, and a quick call to Loftus Depot. 'Take that dog off the bus and send it back here, Albert's got his dog.' The animal was duly returned to Whitby, 'OCS', had the label removed, and released to go on its way.

Maybe the greatest regret to a historian is that Charlie Dickinson's memories were not recorded. He started with Amos, Proud at Choppington, went to United on take over, aged twenty two, and spent his working life with them, retiring in 1971 as Traffic Manager. He lived through all the takeovers, witnessed purchase agreements, etc. He had a phenomenal memory. It was always, 'ask Charlie Dickenson, he was there at the time.' The moral is, 'write it down before it's too late.'

16. BUS SERVICES IN THE SCOTTISH BORDERS

Since the 1930s Scottish Motor Traction and its successors, Scottish Omnibuses, Eastern

Paper destination blinds hinder visibility from this Maudslay, K2. SMT had just started to run from Edinburgh to Berwick in 1928 and had a new bus for it. *(R.Grieves)*

Scottish, etc., have been the main operator north of the Border. It was not always thus so one needs to go further back into history.

There were some 'small men' running into Berwick from the north in the 1920s, at the same time as Spowart, Thompson and Young were running. These were generally taken over by Brook & Amos or SMT thus the best place to start is with: -

BROOK & AMOS

There has been much reference in the book already to AMOS, PROUD who came from Choppington, Northumberland. They have nothing to do with BROOK & AMOS who came first into being through HARRY BROOK, one of the entrepreneurs of his day. He came from Holmfirth, worked as a bus driver with a small operator in Bedlington, then set up AMBLE & DISTRICT in April 1922. Amble & District went very soon into the hands of the Knox family at Amble and Harry Brook moved to Galashiels.

Now prior to the 1914-18 War, Adam Scott, from Yarrow, had set up BORDER BUSES in the Selkirk area. When Adam Scott died, HARRY BROOK took over the Border Buses business. In September 1923, together with the AMOS BROTHERS, James and Willie; with Walter Bryson, and with Robert Knox of Amble,

set up BROOK & AMOS LTD. with a capital of £9000.

Harry Brook's involvement with Brook & Amos was short-lived as, in 1924, he moved to Stranraer, setting up there as Harry Brook & Co. He sold that outfit to the newly formed Caledonian Omnibus Co. in 1927, moving on again to run buses elsewhere in Ireland and England.

So, from 1924, Brook & Amos continued without the Brook part. They had started with ten buses running between Galashiels, Selkirk, Melrose, Walkerburn, etc. and nothing to do with Berwick. Very soon they took over GEORGE HENDERSON, of Duns, who had been running into Berwick from Duns and from Coldingham. That brought four or five charabancs of assorted manufacture, and premises at Coldingham and Chirnside into the business. It established Brook & Amos in Berwick in 1924. They continued to expand both bus services and tours, taking over a number of other operators in the Borders and, by 1926, they had forty-three buses. In April 1926 they were bought by SMT. Concurrently, Adam Purves, of Galashiels, was bought by SMT and put into the Brook & Amos operation, giving them a total of fifty buses.

By this time the Brook & Amos name and its maroon livery had strength and SMT decided to

Eyemouth Old Men's Picnic, Midsummer 1927. The Leyland charabanc, TA731, belongs to Brook & Amos. The location is Selkirk and the driver Alex Munro, of Selkirk. The sail hoisted by the fishermen is not a reflection on the state of the vehicle. All the men come from old Eyemouth families, Collin, Dougal, Lough, etc., and all have nicknames. There are Tam Wallop, Nellie Wullie, Tinney's Bob, Seabreeze, Charlie Geng, etc. The bus dates from 1921.

Turnbull's Motor Service, Kelso owned this Albion PM28, KS 3763, looking new under leafless trees after delivery in 1926. It would soon be in SMT colours as fleet number A86 when SMT took Turnbull's over. The bus was sold in 1935 and converted to a lorry. Even by 1927 standards it looks dated. *(R.Grieves)*

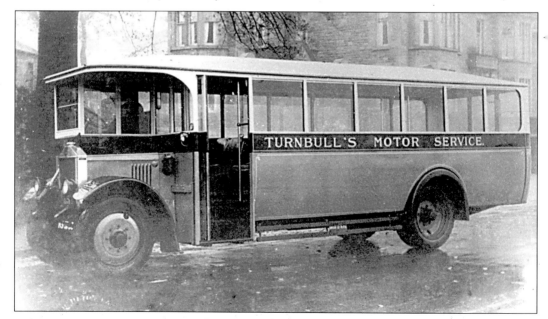

keep the newly acquired business under its existing name. Of the Amos brothers, James went on to become Traffic Manager and, later, Chairman of SMT. Willie remained in charge at Galashiels. The SMT continued to buy small operators in the Borders placing them into the Brook & Amos fleet.

By January 1927 there was a service from Allanton to Berwick and the former Henderson service from Coldingham to Berwick had been extended to St.Abbs. By August 1927 they had direct services from Edinburgh to Galashiels and Selkirk, later extended to Hawick, and from Edinburgh to Jedburgh. The latter would soon run through to Newcastle, joint with United.

A major acquisition was that in December 1927 of JOHN TURNBULL, of 35, Bowmont Street, Kelso. Turnbull, whose garage stood where the Bus Station is now, had a haulage business. They had their first new bus in 1922, developing services from Kelso to Edinburgh; to Jedburgh and to Berwick, the latter worked by two big charabancs. Their early buses were 32 seaters but they also bought some of the usual 14 seater Reos and Chevrolets which had the advantage of the higher permitted speed. Later purchases were again of the large capacity and they had fourteen buses when they sold out. Both the nature of their services and their bus fleet, with Albions of the type that SMT were themselves buying, made it an important purchase.

With the take over of Turnbull and the others in 1927, SMT saw fit to place all the Borders services under the SMT name in 1928, although the Brook & Amos company was not wound up until 1934. There was another purchase by SMT shortly after shedding the Brook & Amos name. That was JAMES FAIRBAIRN, 15, Oven Wynd, Kelso, whose business was taken over during or after July 1929. It seems he was not long in business, having bought an Albion bus new in March 1929 and having a Hackney Carriage Licence granted by Berwick Borough in April 1929. He ordered two more Albion coaches which were delivered to SMT. He had a service from Kelso to Berwick.

There is a problem with Hackney Carriage Licences in Berwick. In theory, local Councils granted these licences before the 1930 Road Traffic came into force, i.e. 1st January 1931. In practice, some were more scrupulous than others

in issuing them; the large towns and cities more so. Berwick Town Council Minutes list the grant of licences to operate buses and licences for bus drivers and conductors - but by no means all of each. Licences to store petrol were issued in the period 1920-1922. In respect of buses none appear until December 1923 when George Henderson got a licence for a 14-seater bus without indicating where it would run.

Spowart and Thompson, who were running by that time, had no licences listed until later after which they appeared regularly in Minutes, as did their drivers and conductors whose licences were renewed annually. Most other operators' names did not appear other than, at best, infrequently, although George Henderson, of Duns and Alex. Wait, of Chirnside were appearing in 1930. Neither Brook & Amos nor Turnbull ever appeared in Minutes. The first record of SMT was in October 1929 when licences for sixty-three buses were granted. Had Berwick's records been kept, they would have provided valuable information about the bus services. Henderson, for example, had sold out to Brook & Amos in 1923, yet he got a licence from Berwick in 1930 - why?

Some names from across the Border have not yet been included. LAING, of Coldingham, had a small Albion bus running between Reston Station and Coldingham by about 1908, one of the first in the Borders. By 1911 this service was run by JAMES FRENCH and J.B.CHIRNSIDE, of Coldingham. French continued to run until Reston lost its rail service and he remains in the private hire business today. Mr French had an Albion, new in 1928, whose body was built, unusually, by Chisholm, the local joiner. That was probably the bus I saw twenty years later.

In the same area, W.BLACKIE, of Eyemouth, ran between Eyemouth and Berwick for many years, not selling out to SMT until 1934.

I was lucky to get some of the history from Mr.James Elder. He began as a conductor with Brook & Amos in 1923, going with them to SMT, later as District Superintendent at Berwick then Chief Inspector at Edinburgh.

So much for the earlier days, now we have to look at SMT itself. Until 1930 their buses were painted green and cream. In the spring of that year they changed to a blue livery with a cream waistband, retaining it until summer 1949 when they went back to the green livery.

17. SCOTTISH MOTOR TRACTION, SCOTTISH OMNIBUSES, EASTERN SCOTTISH.

I confess to being old-fashioned. In my days of living and working in Berwick we always spoke of 'the SMT'. The Scottish Motor Traction Co. Ltd. was registered in 1905. A new company, Scottish Omnibuses, was registered in 1949. The SMT fleet name was kept until 1961. In 1964 it became Eastern Scottish. Deregulation in 1986 saw the Borders area hived off to a new company, Lowland Scottish, based at Galashiels, back to the old Brook & Amos land. It has changed again, now it is First Edinburgh. It remains SMT to me and I make no apologies for using the name throughout.

My earliest memories are of a shop in Berwick's High Street managed by Marjorie Williams. I must have been at least four years old and intrigued by this large cardboard model of a blue SMT bus in the window. To my regret it had to stay there.

Like United, SMT did not just happen. It has an interesting history which I want to touch on here. The classic work on its history is the late D.L.G.Hunter's book, 'From SMT to Eastern Scottish', published by John Donald for the 80th anniversary.

Scottish Motor Traction was registered on 13th June 1905. In the Prospectus the Directors stated that 'the Motor Bus had been so perfected as to soon supersede the Horse Bus and that there are many routes in Scotland on which it would be more profitable to run Motor Buses than to construct and maintain Tramways'. Their first venture was to run between the Mound and Corstorphine in Edinburgh from January 1906. Routes were developed all around Edinburgh, as well as circular tours by charabanc, this process continuing up to the outbreak of War in 1914. No doubt SMT must have motivated Adam Logan and his partners to start the 'Berwick-on-Tweed Motor Car Co.'

1913 saw another important development. Hitherto the fleet had been largely Maudslay open top double-deckers with a couple of charabancs. These buses had been satisfactory but SMT needed single-deck buses to develop rural services so they designed - and built - their own, calling them Lothian and building almost a hundred. The design was in advance of its time and so satisfactory that many lasted until 1930 - seventeen years - an exceptional life for a bus then , and now.

Expansion continued after 1919 with numerous takeovers, that of Brook & Amos being the big one in the Borders. SMT buses from Edinburgh reached Dunbar early in 1928 and extended on to Berwick on 8th June 1928. This is the time when bus services really came together around Berwick. SMT had buses coming in from Kelso, Duns and St.Abbs; they had come now from Edinburgh; Amos, Proud were running between Newcastle, Berwick and Edinburgh; United were recruiting or transferring staff to Berwick for their Newcastle-Berwick service.

SMT had to find a garage in Berwick so, with United, they kept a bus for their Edinburgh service at Boston's Yard, Sandstell Road, Spittal. Both moved later to the A&B Garage in Silver Street, Berwick; United buses at one end, SMT at the other. SMT did not stay there long, moving to the former Cattle Market behind Chisam's Garage at the corner of Castlegate and Northumberland Avenue. The latter street has always been an 'upmarket' residential area and the residents were not enthused with buses parking, not in the garage area, but on their road. In September 1930 the Council told SMT to stop parking there. They had no office in Berwick and appointed Marjorie Williams at 30, High Street as their Agent, a job she did until the Bus Station opened, having moved in 1931 to 88, High Street.

Bus stops were generally in High Street, starting at the Town Hall and going up the right hand side. SMT had those farthest from the Town Hall for journeys starting at Berwick. Some of the other bus stops were badly sited by today's standards. Some buses stopped in Castlegate below Scott's Place where the pedestrian crossing is now, Others stopped on High Street, just inside Scotsgate. Although the SMT had buses garaged at Chisam's in Berwick they retained one bus each at Duns, Chirnside and Coldingham until Berwick Bus Station opened when they were moved there. James Elder was the first SMT driver at Coldingham He was sent from Galashiels in 1927 to take over the operation from Fisher's Brae garage there returning to Gala a year or so later. His conductor was Fred Voase from Foulden. Late

Girls in 1920s fashions, drivers in leather leggings, passengers in plus fours give away this 1928 scene at Berwick's Scotsgate. The bus on the wrong side of the road, creating a traffic hazard, is SC 1170, a Maudslay ML3B, new to SMT in 1928 as fleet number 664, later K12. No destination blind but a lot of paper bills. One reads 'Newcastle' but passengers had to change at Berwick. *(R.Grieves)*

The same spot 40 years later - not a bus stop in sight. *(P.M.Battersby)*

two crews were based at Coldingham; drivers Basil Crosby and Jimmy Wright and conductresses Cis Thompson and Peg Swanston. These crews also worked part of the Edinburgh service, but only as far as Dunbar, where they changed over with an Edinburgh crew. Cis Thompson (Mrs.Voase) was the first conductress in Berwickshire. James Elder returned to Berwick in 1930, working the joint Newcastle-Edinburgh service with United.

Based at Blythe's Garage at Chirnside were drivers Andrew Lauder and Tom Chapman and conductresses Nan Walker (Mrs.Slater) and Nancy Hattle. At Duns were drivers Jock Spiden and Bill Souter, conductors Bobby Flynn and Jimmy Spence and conductress Jenny Summers. Most, if not all, of these came to work at Berwick.

When Henderson's service from Coldingham was taken over it had some longish layovers in Berwick. As that bus was blocking shops in High Street, arrangements were made for it to take layover in Wallace Green. Only someone who knows Berwick knows the significance of this, but to get from Wallace Green to the stop on High Street buses went down Church Street, turning right at the Town Hall into High Street. The tight right turn at the Town Hall was not satisfactory so the next route agreed by the Council, Police and SMT was that buses would leave Wallace Green, going along the Parade, down Ravensdowne and Woolmarket into High Street. At least that got rid of the right turn at the Town Hall but Ravensdowne is narrow and today 'residents access only.'

By the early 1930s SMT had established its position as the prime operator into Berwick from the north. The final moves were when they took over GARDINER, of Leitholm in 1932, and, in 1934, the Eyemouth-Berwick service run since the 1920s by WILLIAM BLACKIE, of Eyemouth. Blackie's drivers were Jock Nesbitt who came to the SMT at Berwick, and J.Windram. Incidentally, their name is spoken locally as Blaikie,and not as spelt.

SMT buses to Berwick from Edinburgh started, at first, from Waterloo Place, moving soon to the St.Andrew's Square terminal, without passenger shelter, which they used until the Bus Station opened in 1957.

As well as the service on the A1, United and SMT teamed up to run through services from Edinburgh to Newcastle via Jedburgh in 1928, and via Kelso and Wooler in 1929, both routes obtained by buying out others. SMT also ran through from Hawick to Berwick.

United had always used numbers for their services. In 1934 SMT introduced them. The Edinburgh-Newcastle services carried numbers 230, 231, 232 for routes via Berwick (United 12); 270 for the Jedburgh route (United 9); 273 for that via Kelso and Wooler (United 15). Services in the Borders had numbers prefixed by 'B', B8, Galashiels-Berwick; B51/52, Berwick-St.Abbs, etc. While these numbers appeared in timetables, many buses did not carry route number blinds so numbers did not always appear. What SMT did have, traditionally, were paper bills stuck on the windows listing the principal places en route.

SMT START A TOWN SERVICE IN BERWICK.

The pattern of services on the north side was now set with SMT as the sole operator. The first big change in Berwick was a new service from High Street to the 'North Road Housing Scheme', then colloquially known as 'Abyssinia.'

By the 1920s, and the prospect of 'homes fit for heroes' following the War, Berwick's housing stock, with its rabbit warren of yards, was not in sparkling condition. New Council houses had been built towards the end of the decade around the south side of the New Bridge; Blakewell Gardens was built in 1931-1932, but the need for housing was still extreme.

Tenders were accepted in October 1934 for the first 100 houses on land east of the A1 along the North Road, let a year later. More were to be built and in February 1936 the Council decided it would be known as 'Highfields'. Now Mussolini had just had his war in Ethiopia, then known as Abyssinia. That estate never got anything else but 'Abyssinia' for years. I doubt if some of the residents knew it as anything else. There would be a repetition in 1938 when the Billendean Estate was built. That was the time of the Hitler crisis over the Sudetenland in Czechoslovakia. That estate got the name 'Czechoslovakia', later shortened to 'the Checks.'

Having disposed of that totally irrelevant piece of social history, SMT began a service to the so-

VF 7666, United's Leyland Tiger TS3 with fleet number AT102, was new in 1930. The SMT conductress travelling home on it is Cis Thompson (Mrs Voase), the first conductress in Berwickshire, based at Coldingham.

The youthful crew of this SMT Albion, SF 7149, are Jimmy Elder (20) and Fred Voase (15). The bus was new in January 1927 as fleet number 541, later A40. In this 1927 photo it was based at Coldingham, working the St Abbs - Berwick service. To avoid blocking the shops in High Street, layover was taken at Wallace Green, where it stands in this picture. Both men spent their working lives with SMT.

called 'North Road Housing Scheme' not long after the houses were built. At first it was hourly, increased to half hourly in the evening. That was for cinema traffic. Berwick had two cinemas then, the Theatre and the Playhouse, better known as 'the Top Hoose' and 'the Bottom Hoose.' You could always get a bus for the 'first hoose', i.e. from about 6.15pm to 8.00pm. If you went to the 'second hoose', you had to walk home. The programmes always changed midweek so you could - and did - go four times a week. I never did understand why the United and SMT did not stretch their last buses to cope with the 'second hoose.'

However, back to Highfields. The service ran at first from High Street, moving to the Bus

Station when it opened. As more houses went up, the hourly service was increased to half hourly, with a 20 minute evening service. Like everything else, the service was reduced during the War, returning to a similar level when fuel restrictions were lifted. That situation stayed until the services to Spittal and to Highfields were linked in 1947 to make a cross-town service every 15 minutes. Two United buses and one SMT worked it, the SMT allocation was always AEC B181, BSC 518.

In my time in Berwick, 1950, the conductors didn't like working the late buses to Highfields. United crews did the 10.18pm from Golden Square, SMT did the last bus at 10.33pm. There was always trouble with passengers trying to avoid paying, the biggest problem was with those who got on at 'Mabel's in Castlegate. Berwick was not subject to too many problems with drunks, but a retired conductress related an incident to me. This was on Prior Park town service, not Highfields. 'I had a drunk man on my bus.' 'He was always drunk'. 'I couldn't get him off the bus so the driver came round to the door, heaved him on to his shoulder, and draped him over the hedge!'

After the War, when passenger traffic was at its maximum, some new services were introduced by SMT but, as did others, they still ran many elderly buses. One such, working regularly between Kelso and Berwick, was SMT Leyland H1, SC 3351, new in 1929, not withdrawn until 1954, then passing to a contractor. It had a distinctive engine sound entering the bus station.

The 8th April 1949 saw a change in the Company's constitution. Having been sold to the British Transport Commission, the erstwhile SMT's interests in motor sales, etc. were separated and the bus operations put in the hands of a new company, Scottish Omnibuses Ltd. By agreement, the fleet name 'SMT' was continued for some years. James Amos, one of the founders of Brook & Amos in 1923, became Chairman of the new company. He retired in 1963, a legend in road transport circles.

A little bit now on the lighter side. Kirk Yetholm is just in Scotland. Apart from being the end of the Pennine Way and having had Stenhouse's buses, it has another claim to fame. In 1695, one Captain Bennett settled gipsies there in return for services rendered. As well as being 'muggers' and 'horners' (their gipsy trades) they were a bit of a tourist attraction in the 19th century and they had their own 'King', 'Coronation', Gipsies Palace and other trappings. Also at Kirk Yetholm lived Richie Stenhouse, not one of the bus operating family, but a bus driver with SMT from before the War until retiring in 1967. Richie was on an outing to the seaside taking women, children and pushchairs. At the destination, unloading pushchairs from the back locker, he put a half crown between his teeth. His 'mate' said, 'ye shudna pit that in yer mooth, its durrty.' 'Ah've pit it therr tae let them think somebody's gaen me a tip, an' thae'll think thae'll hae tae gie me yin an' a'!' From Kelso Square buses can use one of two parallel streets to get to Berwick. This day Richie asked his conductress, 'which way dae we go?'. A woman passenger heard the question and said to the conductress, 'ay, daes the driver no' ken the way? - ah'd better git oot!'

SMT ran the Berwick-Kelso buses. Another digression, not a lot to do with the buses except that a Mr.Skelly lived a bit out of Berwick on the Canty's road and used the Kelso bus to come in and out of the town years ago. One of the old-time barbers in Berwick was Jock Burgon, 'Jock the Barber', who had a little shop down West Street. He was one of the town's characters, still in business in the 1950s. You could sit ankle deep in cut hair, hearing all the local news and wait interminably for a haircut. I know, I always went there. Now Jock was also a prankster. One afternoon Mr.Skelly was waiting his turn for a haircut and a boy was waiting for the turn before him. Jock knew Mr.Skelly wanted the 3 o'clock Kelso bus but time was running out. Jock asked the boy if Mr.Skelly could go in front of him. No way, he had sat there long enough. Nothing more was said for a few minutes until Jock said to the lad, 'had away ti' the P'lice Station, son, an' ask if therr open oan Christmas Day!.' The lad got as far as the door, turned round and said, 'ya hevvin me oan, Mr.Burrgin'. Mr.Skelly didn't get the lad's turn or the 3 o'clock bus. Older readers might remember being sent for 'the long stand'.

18. 1948 - AND THE FLOODS

We are fortunate not to get too many extremes of weather. There were heavy snowfalls in 1940 and 1947, the East Coast floods of January 1953

Just arrived in New Street, Edinburgh from Berwick is AEC Regal B182, BSC 519. Its mate, B181, worked Berwick - Spittal for years. It is of 1934 vintage with Alexander body. *(R.Grieves)*

Nearing the end of its life with SMT is SC 2091, a 1928 Star Flyer with Hoyal body. N26 was photographed at Yetholm in 1934. SMT had just taken over the Kelso - Yetholm service from John Stenhouse, allocating this bus to the out-station. The driver is Richie Stenhouse.

and the local floods of 1948. In a normal August the Borders might expect about 4 inches of rain. In 1948, August had 10.5 inches in total, of which 5 or 6 inches fell in the deluge of 11/12th. It is still clear in my memory.

I was home on leave and, ignorant of what might be, set off by bus for Edinburgh. The rivers and burns were in spate everywhere but when we reached Heughhead Smithy we were not prepared for what we saw. From there to Grantshouse the railway, often visible on our left, had been destroyed. Seven or eight railway bridges had been washed away, leaving the lines hanging in mid air. On our right the roadside cottages had little rivers running into their back doors and out the front. We could hardly get off the bus in the midst of this chaos; better to stay where we were and, if necessary, we could stay in Edinburgh. We did manage to get back that day but the journey was a nightmare with even more damage along the route as the rain had persisted all day.

This is what happened. There was this immense rainfall on the Lammermuirs and the Cheviots. The water ran down quickly to the usually small Eye Water which flows on the landward side of the railway line. There, the embankments held the water back until it formed a lake thirty-five feet deep behind the railway. In the process the torrents coming off the hills carried trees, animals and everything else with them. With the sheer weight against the stonework many bridges gave way. Thankfully, the embankment held otherwise the flood down the Eye Water would have inundated Eyemouth. Apart from the broken bridges there was a landslide at Grantshouse. South of Berwick there was damage to the railway track at Scremerston and water reached the platform level a Belford. Passengers from the 'Flying Scotsman' had to be transhipped to buses at Goswick Station. Main line trains, unable to get north from Berwick, were diverted along the single track from Tweedmouth to Kelso and St.Boswells and on to

ESC 448, SMT B254, was one of a batch of early post-war AEC Regals, delivered in 1946. This one was working a private hire from Cranshaws to Portobello in August 1948. With serious flooding in the area it reached Millburn Bridge near Duns. The driver, Bob Grant, from Berwick, was driving slowly over when the bridge began to collapse under him. Thanks to his prompt action everybody escaped unhurt other than for shock.

Edinburgh. The main line remained closed until late October 1948.

What about bus services? In Berwickshire fifteen bridges were totally destroyed and many others damaged. The A1 was closed for two days at Syphon Bridge, Cockburnspath. Doddington Bridge and Canty's Bridge were destroyed and eventually replaced by Bailey bridges, themselves lasting for many years before permanent replacements were built. In all thirty-two buses were stranded in Berwick on that Thursday night. We were lucky to have got back from Edinburgh in one piece.

The nearest thing to a bus disaster happened at Millburn Bridge. Two SMT buses from Berwick had set out for Portobello with members of a Ladies' Guild from Cranshaws and Abbey St.Bathans. Returning, the first bus reached Millburn Bridge when the bridge began to collapse underneath it, leaving the bus hanging over the gap. There were some minor injuries and only prompt action by the driver, Bob Grant, saved the situation. Another Berwick SMT bus en route from Galashiels to Berwick was halted at Chirnside Bridge. Driver Willie Short warned the passengers, many of whom left the bus to cross on foot. Willie drove the bus over in safety.

With the railway out of action between Berwick and Dunbar there was a combination of rail and bus services north of the Border. Buses linked the railheads at Tweedmouth and Dunbar. SMT Kelso had particular problems as so many bridges were unusable in their area. Their saving grace was that the schools were on holiday and they had spare buses.

Bob Welsh, the gamekeeper for Abbey St.Bathans Estate, told me, 'Our house was down near the river. As the water rose we began to worry and in time we had to climb out on to the roof. We had an infant and an elderly man with us. The coastguards were contacted and a breeches buoy brought in to get us off the roof not long before the house collapsed.' That is the only time that a breeches buoy has been used inland and not for a shipwreck.

North Northumberland was also badly affected. Norham, for example, was swamped within a few hours as the water rose so quickly.

Many of the efforts of the bus crews went unrecorded but Rev. James Cowley of Coldingham paid tribute to them publicly, 'they stood up to the strain in an admirable way.'

19. BERWICK'S OLD BRIDGE

Until 1928 the sole crossing of the Tweed at Berwick was the Tweed Bridge, more commonly known as the Old Bridge. It is a superb stone structure built to the orders of James I and opened in 1627. Its width varies between 17' and 19'. With a narrow footway on each side the carriageway is no more than 14' wide near the Berwick end.

Until the so-called New Bridge was opened on 16th May 1928, the Old Bridge carried the A1 London-Edinburgh road and all traffic, cars, buses, lorries, horses and carts and all pedestrians. The next realistic crossing was at Coldstream, fifteen miles up river. That at Chain Bridge was only suitable for light traffic and Norham Bridge did not offer a convenient traffic route.

The Old Bridge always carried signs asking pedestrians to keep to the right and, in general, local people did. It never crossed my mind to walk on 'the wrong side', nor do I to this day.

I have quite a wide car, c.5'6" wide and I have to take care when passing on the Bridge. But the buses and lorries were wider than that. Not until 1st January 1931 when the 1930 Road Traffic Act came into force were there universal regulations as to the construction of buses and a maximum width of 7'6" was introduced. By the late 1920s the big companies, Leyland for example, were building their 'Tiger' buses at 26' long and 7'4" wide. Early charabancs had rows of four seats without a central gangway but even then they would be at least 6'6" wide. The small buses with 14 to 20 seats had a central gangway and would be about 7' wide. Imagine the problems of vehicles passing each other, and of passing horses, given a carriageway 14' wide.

By 1925 the Town Council was concerned about traffic on the Old Bridge. Local buses were still small, but wide enough to be a traffic hazard. Council Minutes for 29th September 1925 record that Spowart and Thompson were authorised to operate three 20 seater buses each on services to Spittal and Scremerston. The Council required buses not to exceed 5mph on both Bridge Street and the Old Bridge. They had no means of enforcing those limits. What does not appear is any restriction on any other operator. At the time John Young had services to Norham and Wooler, and Knox ran to Alnwick.

Berwick's 'New Bridge' looks new c.1928/29. The brochure for its opening says of the Old Bridge 'that motor transport rendered its narrow roadway dangerous. To widen it would have been difficult and might have mutilated an historic monument of great interest and beauty.' Buses were still using the Old Bridge. This one, belonging to Spowart Bros, hasn't much room to pass the handcart. The road sign left of the entrance displays the traffic restrictions. Pedestrians are 'keeping to the right' as instructed. *(R.Grieves)*

No doubt it stemmed from the rivalry between Spowart and Thompson.

By 1927 the New Bridge was under construction and Amos, Proud had started to run through from Newcastle to Edinburgh. They used Leyland PLSC 'Lions' and 'Tiger' TS1s and TS2s - full width buses i.e.7'4" wide. They started from High Street via Hide Hill and Bridge Street but it was not unknown for a driver to go down West Street.

Once the New Bridge opened in 1928 there were attempts to reduce the use of the Old Bridge by buses. There was a great deal of debate locally and moves either to close the Old Bridge to traffic or make it one-way. Bridge Street traders were not unanimous in their views but one-way traffic was not generally favoured. One trader thought that the alteration to traffic would cost extra cartage and - 'to make horses drag up Hide Hill on a surface made for motorists was not cricket'. None wanted to see the Spittal buses taken off the Old Bridge.

The 'Berwick Journal' took a traffic census on both bridges on 23rd and 26th May 1928, but only half an hour each day. In total, 59 vehicles crossed the New Bridge and 57 the Old Bridge in the two half hours recorded. Private cars had moved to the New Bridge, lorries and horses and carts had not.

Matters culminated in a Draft Order coming into force in November 1930. This placed a maximum of 14 seats on 'Heavy Motor Cars' with various other traffic restrictions, which used to appear on the diamond-shaped plates at each end of the Bridge. The Road Traffic Act of 1930, which totally changed the concept of bus operation, would come into force two months later.

Given the infinite wisdom of hindsight it was not an entirely wise move. Neither Spowart nor Thompson had enough 14 seater buses to meet the conditions; Spowart had only two and Thompson, one. Remember that the Town Council had authorised the use of 20 seater buses in 1925 and both operators had bought accordingly. Furthermore, public opinion favoured the Old Bridge route and 20 seaters gave a better load factor. However the writing must have been on the wall. Spowart had bought a 20 seater as late as February 1928; Thompson bought a 26 seater Albion in May 1927 and a 25 seater in February 1928. Spowart did not buy a 14 seater until August 1929 and Thompson not until 1931. They had their viability to consider. Buses to Spittal via the Old Bridge started from Sandgate at that time and were very popular. Hitherto it had been a walk to the Quayside for the ferry, so Sandgate was a benefit.

On reflection one might think that the New Bridge with its easy driving conditions, no traffic hazards and its proximity to the High Street would have caused the Spittal operators to want to run that way, but not so. Motorists and High Street shopkeepers feared that extra buses on High Street 'would cause congestion' - i.e. prevent shoppers parking outside the shop doors.

Only on 12th August 1930 did Spowart seek to run a new service to Spittal via the 'High road', asking that no other licence be granted, i.e. , not to Thompson, the 'High Road' being that via Main Street and Billendean as is run now. Spowart got the service but not the monopoly, Thompson getting a similar licence. So, there were the two ways to Spittal. Spowart and Thompson sold to United in 1934; United kept the Old Bridge service until enforced closure by wartime fuel restrictions in 1939.

The Draft Order had a weakness in that the restriction on 'Heavy Motor Cars' related only to seating capacity, not width or weight. In fairness to United, they carried on running 14 seaters as long as possible. But these buses were built for the competitive conditions of the 1920s. The monopoly conditions of the 1930s had little need of them. United found a solution - run bigger buses but take some seats out. They had taken over some Bedford WLB types, more reliable than the 1920s 'chasers', and for which spares were readily available. They drafted into Berwick their fleet nos. SB3 (JR 508) and SB4 (UP 7855). These buses had been taken into the United fleet when George Morton, of Newbiggin, and Mrs.Vasey, of Meadowfield, Durham, respectively, sold out to United in 1933. Both were new that year. Both were 20 seaters, out came six seats, and they ran to and from Spittal until the service was withdrawn in 1939. The Draft Order said 'no more than 14 seats' and that is what they had!.

Berwick was not the only place with 'small bus' conditions for United. Alnwick depot ran Alnwick-Amble via Guyzance, on Saturdays only. There was a seating restriction on a bridge on that route. Being a Saturday only operation it was totally uneconomic for United to keep a small bus just for that. I believe they took seats out of a 35 seater to meet the restriction.

That was not quite the end of the small bus story. In June 1939 suggestions were made that 20 seater buses of not more than either 2½ or 3 tons in weight be operated. The Police would not agree the heavier of the two weights and United had no buses of the lighter, so the matter was dropped. That was the first mention of 'weight' instead of 'seating capacity'. But in another few months the War would see the end of buses on the Old Bridge.

The end of the 20th century has seen all the old arguments about the Old Bridge traffic revived. They were not new in the 1920s. James Good, in publishing his 'Directory of Berwick' in 1806, wrote, 'but from the increase of traffic, the passage is generally allowed to be too narrow : if ten feet were added to its breadth, as has been done both at Newcastle bridge and at Rippon (sic) in Yorkshire, it would be a great improvement and of general utility.' Good's Directory was published in facsimile form by Berwick History Society in 1999. Their work is acknowledged.

It seems that, in respect of traffic problems on the Old Bridge, not a lot has changed between 1800 and 2000.

20. BERWICK-SPITTAL BUS SERVICE

I decided to include a chapter on the Berwick-Spittal service because of its interesting history. In the competitive days of the 1920s it was almost a bit of the 'wild west'. This was the Spowart/Thompson era.

Strictly speaking they were not the first; Adam Logan and his 'Berwick-upon-Tweed Motor Car Co. Ltd' was first with a limited service from August 1913. The other options were to walk or take the ferry from Berwick Quayside to Spittal's Little Beach. That ferry, about which more later, was owned at some time by Adam Logan and bought by Spowart in 1907.

How it all began has been lost with the passage of time. THOMPSON BROS., Robert, Andrew and Hector, of Scremerston, set up as hauliers in 1912, running motor and steam lorries and building up a substantial business. We know from vehicle records that Thompsons bought a 16 seater Albion bus (NL 4614) in March 1923. Where they started to run their bus is not known. They did run from Berwick both to Scremerston and to Spittal, and may well have been the first to have a regular service to Spittal. The Albion was followed by another four buses in due course, in a green livery with black roof. Unlike most bus operators who give buses individual fleet numbers, or just use the registration number, Thompsons gave theirs names of letters of the Greek alphabet: - Alpha, Beta, Gamma, Delta and Epsilon (sic). Robert Thompson, as well as a road haulier, was also an Olympic standard cyclist, competing in 1924.

SPOWART BROS. bought their first bus in May 1923, an 18 seater GMC (NL 4905). It proved so successful they bought a second bus in July 1923, a Karrier 14 seater (NL 5731). Philip and Robert Spowart came from an old Spittal family with seafaring connections. In 1907 they bought the Spittal ferry which provided the normal means of transport to and from Spittal until the buses came in 1923. Spowart continued to run the ferry after the bus service began,

keeping it until 1939 despite having sold the buses to United in 1934. Spowart's tickets were interchangeable between their red buses and the ferryboats.

Going back to 1923 no official records exist. Drivers and conductors were licensed by the Town Council who also gave approval for the running of individual bus services. That approval was often no more than for 'a licence for a....seater bus for hire.' Council Minutes dated September 1925 authorise both Spowart and Thompson to operate two 20 seater buses between Berwick and Spittal and one 20 seater each between Berwick and Scremerston and 'not to exceed 5mph on Bridge Street and the Old Bridge.' In September 1926 Spowart was allowed four buses and Thompson three buses for Spittal, that permission granted for a year.

Detailed timetables as we know them now did not always exist in the 1920s outside the big companies like United who were meticulous in providing them. Only with the advent of the 1930 Road Traffic Act did operators have to produce detailed timetables for approval by the Traffic Commissioners.

TY 7951, a Chevrolet LQ 14-seater new to Spowart Bros in 1930, takes a break at Spittal terminus.

In 1928 the Town Council approved the Berwick-Spittal bus service as: -

Monday-Friday: - 11.30am to 10.15pm, 2 buses from each firm.
Saturday: - 10.30am to 5.40pm, 2 buses from each firm. 5.40pm to 10.0pm, 3 buses from each firm.

Two buses per firm gave a bus every 7-8 minutes; three buses gave a 5 minutes service.

In 1929 the Town Council authorised an increased frequency: -

Monday-Friday: - 10.0am to 10.15pm, a basic 7-8 minutes service but, 'it could be increased to 5 minutes when required.'
Saturday: - from 10.0am, all day, a 5 minutes service, and 'the service could start earlier if required.'
Sunday: - 2.0pm to 6.0pm, every 15 minutes.
6.0pm to 10.0pm, every 7-8 minutes, and 'the 7-8 minutes service to start at 2.0pm if required.'

Buses started from Sandgate, Berwick and from the Blenheim Hotel, Spittal.

In approving the frequencies quoted above the Town Council were trying to be fair to both operators. But fairness would be difficult to achieve. Given that the two firms were 'daggers drawn' who decided a fair arrangement when the service was permitted to be increased?

Since Thompsons were the first to buy a bus, they may have been first to run the Spittal service, in which case they must have felt they had the prior right. Spowart had been running the ferry for sixteen years, the main means of travel to and from Spittal, so they, too, wanted the monopoly.

Right from the start there was intense rivalry between Thompsons and Spowarts drivers. I am told that buses passed each other along the Dock Road at the old Malthouse, i.e. opposite the Boat Inn Bank. Before the Malthouse was destroyed by fire in 1935, the road there was quite narrow. It was common for drivers to force the opposition bus into the wall, scratching the paintwork or maybe causing minor body damage. Drivers were accused of blocking each other's buses at the terminus and of every conceivable nuisance. It is said they settled scores along the Spittal Promenade, too.

Apart from Sandgate and the Blenheim Hotel, there were no official bus stops and that caused trouble. A letter to the 'Berwick Journal' in 1928 read, 'On Saturday night I saw two buses racing round Bridge Street corner to get away first to Spittal. Fortunately at the time there were no other vehicles at the corner otherwise there might have been an accident, and I do think official stopping places should be made. They pull up anywhere, on corners, in the middle of the street, and without any warning to following vehicles. It is high time the Police took steps in this matter.'

The paper carried another letter in similar terms:- 'the facts are, at the above time stated (10.30pm) a bus which had first call on the road was about to depart for Spittal when, suddenly, an opposition bus steals up from behind, passing right in front, standing for some time blocking the streets in all directions.'

The Police had already taken steps in this matter. A driver for one firm appeared on a charge of 'having driven a motor bus in a manner dangerous to the public at Main Street, Tweedmouth' earlier in 1928. Witnesses' statements in Court were contradictory but the driver was found 'Guilty' and fined £5.00 and costs. On that occasion the Chairman said he hoped it would be a severe warning to all drivers of the two firms. 'The drivers on one side were as much to blame as on the other.' As a member of the Council he knew they continually had complaints of the conduct of the buses and he hoped the owners would see that the drivers in future would not take risks to the public. Strong words - but they continued to fall on deaf ears. One finds constant reference to problems of one sort or another.

Back in 1925 the Town Council authorised the service to Spittal with the proviso that the buses were not to exceed 5mph on Bridge Street and the Old Bridge. In 1926 the Council appointed Mr.R.W.Smeaton, the Borough's Inspector of Weights and Measures, to 'act as Inspector of Omnibuses'. What, if anything, he could do is not apparent but he did report on the need for a handle on the inside of the emergency door of each bus.

The irregularities continued. The Inspector of Hackney Carriages reported to the Works

Committee on 23rd July 1929 on the irregular running of Thompson's buses. On 17th June 1930, a new summer timetable having been authorised, Spowarts were warned to adhere to the timetable otherwise the licence would not be renewed. Thompsons were warned similarly at the July 1930 Works Committee. At the time Philip Spowart was a Councillor.

Thus in July 1930 life had not changed. Except, of course, that the New Bridge had opened two years earlier despite which Spittal buses stuck to the Old Bridge. But change was in sight. On 12th August 1930 Spowart sought to operate a service between High Street and Spittal via the New Bridge and 'the High Road', asking that no other licence be granted, i.e. to the opposition. The Council agreed to the service but not to the monopoly. After much argument timetables were fixed and came into operation early in 1931 giving services (a) from Sandgate to Spittal via the Old Bridge and 'the Low Road' and (b) from High Street to Spittal via the New Bridge and Billendean, 'the High Road'.

The role of the Town Council as Licensing Authority ceased on 1st January 1931 with the introduction of the 1930 Road Traffic Act. Traffic Commissioners were appointed to oversee and regulate the industry and life would never be the same again - at least not until 1986 when the bus industry was once again de-regulated.

Meanwhile United were building up a substantial empire in north east England. They had come to Berwick in 1928 and saw possibilities. So in November 1933, apparently unbeknown to each other, both Spowart and Thompson negotiated their sale to United who took them over on the Saturday of the March Hirings 1934. They cost United £3950 and £3850 respectively. But moves were afoot to regulate bus stops in the town centre during the negotiations.

In September 1933 new stops were agreed by which all Spittal buses moved to High Street, taking the stop nearest to the Town Hall, just outside the Berwick Arms. They came into use on 8th November 1933. That did not bring peace. The loss of the Sandgate terminus was the cause of complaints for many months although the Old Bridge service was still going along Bridge Street. Buses were filling up at the Town Hall to the detriment of people waiting at the Bridge

End. One well-known council official, short in stature (and popularity) was waiting there for his dinnertime bus home to Spittal. The conductress had a full bus. 'Haven't you room for a little one? asked the man. 'Son, if th' cut ya legs oaf, ah still wudn't hev room', came the reply.

What happened on Spittal from 1923 to 1931 was the era of competition, repeated all over the country and certainly prevalent in south Northumberland. From the all the reports of irregular running, of buses racing each other, etc. one might believe that the time allowed for the journey was inadequate. In fact, to maintain the timetable, drivers had fifteen minutes to get from Sandgate before return departure time from Spittal i.e. half an hour for the round trip. Given that it is less than two miles, it gives a low average speed. After United took over, the round trip time dropped to twenty minutes, a 33% reduction.

United gave the Spittal services route numbers after take-over; the 'Low Road' became Service 61; the 'High Road', Service 62. The timetable for the summer of 1934 shows a basic twenty minutes service on each route, but the 'Low Road' increased to every ten minutes on Saturdays - a considerable change from the former five minute service. The 'High Road' service was not restricted to small buses and United brought in Bristol JO5G types with 35 seats and standing room. They were the mainstay of the service for many years with fleet nos. BJO 41, 57 and 80 usually running.

As already mentioned the Old Bridge service was withdrawn in 1939 and never reinstated. Service 62 was reduced to half hourly then.

After the War Service 62 was extended from the Blenheim Hotel to the Spa Well, reversing into Spa Well Road.

The next big change to the service came on 6th July 1947 when it was linked with that of the SMT to Highfields, becoming joint between United and SMT and running every fifteen minutes all day.

Passenger traffic levels everywhere reached their peak in the early 1950s and Spittal buses were very busy. The Kelso trip day was especially so. If it were showery then everybody crowded on to the buses and came over to Woolworths, returning when the sun shone. It was hard work for the conductors; evenings being busy with so much picture traffic.

CHN 280, a United Bristol JO5G with fleet number BJO80, usually worked on Berwick - Spittal until transferred to Durham District Services Ltd in 1952. It has just reversed into Spa Well Road, the post-war Spittal terminus. The photo is post-war, the destination blind, which is pre-war, shows an incorrect setting for service 61 'via Old Bridge'. BJO types had 35 seats and thus were never allowed to cross the Old Bridge. *(The Omnibus Society)*

United operated their Berwick town services in the late 1960s with these Bristol KSW6Bs. WHN 56 brightens up the grey houses at Prior Park terminus in October 1968. *(P.M.Battersby)*

The 35 seater single-deckers were partly replaced in 1956 when the first Bristol LS5G type was allocated. These were single-deckers with underfloor engines and 45 seats. Further changes came in the early 1960s when United brought double-deckers to Berwick. Those working on Spittal-Highfields were Bristol with 5-cyl. Gardner engines and 'lowbridge' bodies with 55 seats. The Gardner engines, while extremely sturdy, were the same as fitted to the 35 seat single-deckers and under powered. They were hard work for the drivers. Conductors and passengers suffered too. The lowbridge design had a dropped gangway on one side of the upper deck, lowering the overall height of the bus allowing it to go under low bridges. The dropped gangway meant that the headroom on the offside of the lower deck was quite low, so heads were bumped. On the top deck the seats were in rows of four, inevitably occupied by three people only, and again headroom on all seats upstairs was limited.

These 'lowbridge' deckers were replaced later in the 1960s by deckers with a centre gangway upstairs, i.e. 'highbridge' types. They had 6-cyl. Bristol engines giving more power and an easier life for passengers and crew.

The SMT also introduced double-deckers, AECs, smart in their green livery, but of lowbridge design, then standard SMT practice.

Unlike United, SMT never gave the Spittal-Highfields service a route number for some unknown reason. Their town services and mill services in the Border towns all carried numbers. On 4th January 1965 SMT introduced a new route numbering system throughout. Spittal was given the number 439 with both companies using it.

Double-deckers gave way in time to large single-deckers, rear engined Bristols. The Highfields end was extended to Newfields and the Spittal end diverted to the large housing estate at Highcliffe. Spittal was then left as a separate service run by United.

1986 saw buses de-regulated; United was broken up and Northumbria Motor Services appeared. SMT, too, was broken up, the Borders services becoming Lowland Scottish. Now we had a return to competition, Northumbria's red and grey mini-buses and Lowland's green 'Berwick Beavers' providing buses between Newfields and Highcliffe about every three minutes. The clock had been turned back - nearly - to the former Spowart/Thompson situation. Clearly that could not be sustained and Lowland pulled out of the town services, leaving them to Northumbria. Minibuses to Spittal - this is where we came in!

As a child I travelled on Spowart's and Thompson's buses. I was too young to remember much except this. I stood on the pavement at the Blenheim Hotel terminus at Spittal in front of this little bus. It had a narrow doorway with steep steps. A very fat lady was trying to get out and had become jammed in the narrow doorway. Somebody on the street was trying to pull her out while others inside the bus pushed. Buses were designed by thin people then!

One bit of history I want to bring out is how busy the Spittal bus services were. United records still exist in Durham Record Office so I looked at their traffic receipts for some weeks in 1938. Traffic receipts are the takings calculated from conductors' ticket sales plus, in this case, the sales of 12 journey tickets. United measured them in pence per mile operated, a formula no longer used. The week of 22nd July 1938 was particularly busy. Service 61, the 'Low Road', with 14 seater buses, earned 12.44 pence per mile; Service 62, the 'High Road', with 35 seater buses, earned 17.15 pence per mile.

Berwick to Spittal is near enough two miles and the fare was then 2d, with 1d intermediate and child fares. The average fare would thus be about 1½d. The 'Low Road', giving receipts of 25d per single journey on average with a 1½d fare, would give 16 passengers per journey. Given the small size of the bus, it gives a load factor today's bus operators would welcome. The 'High Road', giving receipts of 34.5d per journey, had an average of 23 passengers per journey. These figures are meaningless unless compared with some of United's 'busy' services. For example, the Stockton-Middlesbrough-Redcar service gave a return of 16d per mile, with double-deckers. By the end of October 1938, receipts on Spittal were down, but so were they on Service 73 - to 11.5d.

This was the heyday of Spittal's popularity.

21. ABOUT BUS TICKETS

Back in days of yore most bus operators used Bell Punch tickets. Conductors (or one man drivers) carried a rack on which were mounted bundles of tickets of each fare denomination, in United's case from 1d to 17/6d, so ticket racks were sizeable. A ticket for the appropriate fare was taken from the rack and punched at the stage number. Staff carried a waybill on which the starting and finishing numbers were entered and from which cash due to the company was easily calculated. The system was simple but cumbersome in that great stocks of tickets had to be held both in offices and by conductors. Cash shortages against tickets issued had to be repaid, and if too often, meant dismissal.

The old Bell Punches fell from favour in the 1930s and, for a time, United used TIM machines on some local routes. They contained a blank paper roll. The fare was selected on a telephone-type dial, the handle turned, and the printed ticket ejected and torn off. They were simple, quick, self-accounting and 'office-friendly'.

United then turned to the universal use of Bell Punch Automaticket machines, sometimes called 'Bellgraphic'. These contained a bundle of not more than 550 tickets, in concertina form, with a blank roll as duplicate and a carbon in between. A blank ticket showed in the aperture at the top of the machine on which conductors had to write the numbers of the stages boarded and to which they were going, and the fare. The handle was depressed and out came the ticket to be torn off carefully. The copy roll went to Newcastle for audit.

There were pitfalls. The ticket clerk - me in 1950 - could be careless. I might be careless with the carbon insert and the machine would jam. Machines had a paper seal to prevent tampering by conductors and could only be refilled in the office. Refills to the machine were joined by a piece of sticky paper (it was the right size!). The joint had to be straight and firm or it would split and the machine would jam. To force more than

550 tickets into the machine was another potential disaster - the machine jammed straight away. But I wasn't the only guilty party. A ham-fisted conductor could jam the handle or rive a ticket out and tear the roll. Possibilities were endless. To cover impending disasters conductors carried emergency tickets. They were even worse. They were books of tickets with a carbon copy, which took an age to write out - bad enough if you were on a country service but diabolical on town buses. 550 tickets would not last a full shift on Spittal so buses had to come into the Bus Station en route for a machine refill. It had to be done in a hurry but too much speed spelt trouble. If the machine was going to break down, sod's law dictated it would happen halfway across the New Bridge on the way to Spittal with a standing load. Having said the machines held 550 tickets, it was not unknown in those days to sell 1000 tickets in one shift.

Automaticket machines were replaced by Setrights in the 1960s. Like the TIM they contained a blank roll but dials on the sides selected fares and stage numbers. They were able to issue a much greater range of fares than the TIM. SMT ceased to use the old Bell Punch

Enjoying the 1939 summer sunshine are Cissie Burgon, Jenny Jamieson and Zena Edgar from Berwick. The bus, either H49 or H50, was one bought by Amos, Proud in 1928 and taken over by United that year. As United had no licences to enter Edinburgh, they painted the buses in SMT livery but used United staff. They were transferred to SMT in April 1929. The girls have Setright insert ticket machines.

in the mid '30s, replacing them with an earlier type of Setright machine, the 'insert-type'. Conductors carried a rack with three kinds of blank tickets, blue for single, red for return, yellow for ½d overprint. The fare and stage were selected on dials at the side, a blank ticket inserted; the handle turned thus printing the information on the blank ticket. SMT crews were used to them but if you didn't tilt the machine up when you turned the handle, the ticket fell out unprinted but with the machine having registered the cash at your expense. The insert type was replaced by the Setright roll type in common with United. Where SMT and United ran joint services i.e. between Newcastle and Edinburgh, all crews used United machines in United 'territory' and SMT machines in SMT area. Thus Alnwick staff who worked the 0934 Alnwick to Edinburgh and return needed a United machine between Alnwick and Berwick and an SMT machine between Berwick and Edinburgh.

As one manning increased other types of machine had to be found leading to today's electronic machines. It isn't nearly so much fun!

22. SPITTAL FERRY

Although strictly outside the scope of a book about buses I have to include something about the ferry, partly because it was part of the transport scene, and partly because it was owned by two of the early busmen in Berwick, Adam Logan and Spowart.

Until about 1842 Spittal was isolated from Berwick by the lack of a direct road. To go along what is now Dock Road there was only a path, impassable at high tide when one had to climb over a large rock. As Spittal had a lot of fishermen they could use their cobles to get to and from Berwick.

A steamer, the 'Mary', was built in 1846 and began a ferry service between Berwick and Spittal charging a penny fare. A Directory for 1847 reports that, 'James Wilson's steamboat operates to Spittal daily.' By then Spittal was a place to which visitors came to 'take the waters' of the Spa Well. There was also an influx of labour employed on building the railway from Newcastle, opened in 1847, and the Royal Border Bridge.

By 1873 there were two steamboats crossing between Berwick and Spittal, giving a half

hourly service during the summer. The 'Mary' was eventually replaced by the 'Susan', well known and much photographed, with her skipper, 'Stapper Tammy', Thomas Elliott. As a digression, he got his name from his habit, approaching the Quay, of stamping on the deck and calling to the Engineer, 'Stap 'er, Tammy'. By 1888 Kelly's Directory shows Thomas Elliott in business as a ferryman but others are listed: - Thomas Buglass, Walkergate; James Cleghorn, East Street; John Reid, West Street and seven in Spittal - George Davison, James Dean, George Douglas, Wm.Robinson, Richard Wood and James Wilkes. Also in 1888 there was 'a conveyance daily between Bridge Street and Spittal', owned by Cockburn Bros.

Moving on to 1906, Kelly reports Thomas Elliott, of Shore House, Spittal, as a 'steam ferry boat owner' and that 'during the summer season a steamboat and several smaller boats run between Berwick and Spittal every few minutes'. By then only one other ferry boat owner was named:- Alexander Robertson, 101, Low Greens. 'Stapper Tammy' sold out to Adam Logan, of 'Berwick on Tweed Motor Car Co. Ltd' fame in 1906.

In 1907 Adam Logan sold the ferry to Spowart Bros., Philip and Robert, the latter being 'sailmaker, oilskin merchant and pleasure boat owner'. Immediately on acquisition Spowarts bought the first motorboat, the 'Border Chief', seating 55 passengers. That was operated under licence from the Harbour Commissioners. In 1909 they added a small motorboat, the 'Border Maid', a 12 seater, another in 1911 and, in 1912, the 'Border Pride'. By then they were the only ferrymen. These boats maintained the service until 1923 when the bus service began, and continued until 1939, albeit on a lesser frequency. Spowarts also ran pleasure boats on the Tweed and had a boathouse adjacent to the BARC boathouse on the New Road.

Berwick Record Office holds 'Regulations applicable to the Motor Ferry Boats of Messrs. Spowart Brothers'. They lay down when and how the ferries will run and maximum fares. From 1st May to 30th September the maximum fare was 1d. In winter it could be doubled.

23. WARTIME AND BEYOND

The beginning of the War in 1939 is still clear to

Off-peak on the Tweed in 1932. The Spowart Bros ferry 'Border Chief' arrives at Spittal.

me. I heard Neville Chamberlain speak without taking in what it would mean, for the next day I was due to go into the First Form of Berwick Grammar School.

From then until May 1940 we had the 'phoney war'. Immediately we had the blackout. Conscription took longer but bus driving was a reserved occupation so some staff did not go into military service. Not that bus driving or conducting was a 'doddle'. Buses were machine-gunned, staff and passengers killed, although, thankfully, not at Berwick. Earlier in the book I recounted some of Ralph Clydesdale's memories. What I did not tell was that he was a bus driver with Venture of Consett. He was driving in Blaydon when a bomb fell nearby, badly damaging his bus and killing a passenger.

Driving in the blackout was a problem. Vehicle lights were masked, allowing only two or three slits of light. It was akin to driving with a pocket torch. There were many road deaths, including my uncle at Christmas 1940.

Around Berwick United vacated the former church at North Sunderland, which they used as a garage due to 'requisition of buses and fuel rationing'. The Army requisitioned buses from United at Berwick. They were painted grey and taken to Ewart Park where troops were stationed. They took troops to anti-invasion defences at Budle Bay, Bamburgh and Embleton. Berwick drivers went with them, sleeping on the buses. This was when the risk of invasion was greatest in July and August 1940. Buses and drivers returned to Berwick in due course.

Service frequencies were reduced with last buses at 9.0pm. The through service from Newcastle to Edinburgh was split at Berwick in 1943 and timetabled in such a way that buses did not connect at Berwick to prevent people from travelling through. The same applied to Service 15, broken at Coldstream, while Service 9, the Jedburgh route, was withdrawn. A new service, 15A, was introduced between Wooler and Milfield Aerodrome between 6.0pm and 10.0pm daily, restricted to Forces personnel.

To reduce fuel consumption some petrol-engined buses were converted to producer gas, the first in 1941. They were not suitable for hilly areas and, because of the flat terrain, only Northallerton had a full allocation of gas buses. United converted 61 in total, three double-deckers, a lorry, a staff car, the rest single-deck buses. Conversions were still taking place in 1943. They were not popular and were reconverted as soon as possible, all being withdrawn by 1945. Berwick had one bus, not always the same one, AR 12 and BH 9 are known to have been allocated.

Most of the buses used the Bellay-type trailer in which anthracite was burnt and from which the gas was produced. The fire had to be lit every morning and put out on return to the depot. They made a series of minor explosions when cooling down. A reserve of petrol was carried to start the engine. These buses required skill by the drivers to keep the fire and the gas supply going. Some knew how to cope with them and could get to Newcastle and back, others did not. The fires

One of United's buses requisitioned by the Army in 1940 to take troops to the coastal defences. Buses were based at Ewart Park and the drivers slept in them. This was a Sunday at Wooler when their families could visit them. From the left: Bob Blaikie, Jack Robson, Albert Todd and John Richardson from Berwick depot.

United converted 59 buses to run on producer gas, mainly in 1943. Berwick had one allocated but no photo has been traced. Northallerton depot, in the picture, had a full allocation of 11 gas buses. The depot was full of choking fumes when they started up. *(United)*

needed a good draught, working well in fine weather but not in wet or murk. They could not climb hills so Heiferlaw Bank and the Lion Bank at Alnwick were problems for Berwick drivers. It seems there was a detour to avoid the latter but one day Albert Todd decided to try the Lion Bank. The bus didn't take the hill at all well. The slower it went the less gas it produced until it stopped. It began to roll back until the trailer came to rest at the kerb. A passenger said to the conductress, 'open the door and let me out'. The reply came, 'had away, son, efter me!'

There were some comical moments, too. Staff had to do fire-watching, especially when there were raids with incendiary bombs.

Mr.Jowett, United's Area Engineer, rang Bill Huntly, the Depot Foreman at Berwick, with instructions. The men who cleaned the buses were well past military age. Bill Huntly sent for one of them, Tommy Purves, the conversation went like this: -

Bill Huntly: 'Tommy, you'll have to learn to drive.'

Tommy: 'Ah divvent want tae learn tae drive, whae says Ah hev tae?'

Bill Huntly: 'Mr.Jowett. You have to learn to drive so you can drive buses out of the garage if there's a fire raid.'

Tommy: 'an' what makes Mr.Jowett think Ah'll be here if there's a fire raid? Ah'll be at the Bridge end - distance lends enchantment to the view.'

I don't think he ever did learn to drive.

Most foods were rationed, a few were not, sausage being one of them. A queue formed at Harry Taylor's shop, the pork butcher on High Street, on certain days. It became a meeting place, leading to the Sausage Queue Club, which lasted long after rationing ended. The Club's leading light was Mrs.Betty Tait. When fuel restrictions were lifted she organised day trips using SMT buses. I went twice; on one we had breakfast at Hawick, dinner at Dumfries and high tea at Moffat. The other took us to Crieff with similar meal arrangements.

Another recollection, not mine, was of conductress Millie Stammas, a great shopper who would disappear when anything was on offer. Her bus was at Alnwick. The driver got no bell to start so went round to the back of the bus to see what was wrong. No Millie - he found her queueing for oranges.

Many Forces personnel were stationed in the area. The Army was in the Magdalene Fields; there were airfields at Winfield, Milfield and Charterhall. This incident happened at Haggerston. One of the soldiers had travelled out from Berwick on her bus and took a fancy to the conductress. The bus went further on; when it returned to Haggerston, here was this soldier waiting with a huge bunch of flowers. 'What am I going to do with these?' She took them and gave half to the driver. The soldier was not seen again for some time. He got seven days detention for stealing flowers from the gardens at Haggerston White Gates.

Signposts were removed to confuse potential invaders. Gordon Wilson, of whom more later, had a brother, newly commissioned in the Army, stationed somewhere down south. He got word that his unit was posted to Ewart Park, Milfield. Nobody knew where the place was nor did they know that Donald Wilson came from Berwick. Donald led the convoy straight to Ewart Park without the help of signposts. It did his standing with his unit no end of good!

Things were not always funny. Buses were fully loaded and could not always carry everybody. Some single-deckers had the pairs of seats taken out and seats fitted around the sides so as to carry many standing passengers. As an 'essential worker' you might get a permit from the Regional Transport Commissioner to board before the rest of the queue. If not, tough!

As well as the 38 United buses requisitioned for the Army, others went for other uses: -

Eleven went as ambulances; 62 were military vehicles; 67 were held in a Special Reserve; 7 were lent to the Northern Ireland Transport Board and a number were lent to London to cover buses lost through bombing. SMT seem to have fared a bit better than United although I do not have as much information for them as for United. They did have some producer gas buses which worked on the flat terrain between Edinburgh and North Berwick.

Apart from all that, spare parts were hard to get, you made, or cannibalised, what you could and new buses were few and far between. How would today's throwaway society cope with that? I doubt they wouldn't!

24. POST WAR PROSPERITY

Things gradually got back to normal although food and fuel continued to be rationed for some time. Bus services returned to their pre-war levels - people had leisure time and wanted to enjoy it. With a lack of private transport they used buses. Forces personnel were still stationed locally; there were Land Army girls, prisoners of war, and 'displaced persons', refugees from Eastern Europe.

The prisoners of wars were housed in a camp at Wooler being taken out by bus daily to work on the farms. Crown Coaches had the contract for that. The D.Ps were different. They were free to move about but could speak little or no English. They always looked 'lost' - little wonder.

There was a bus from Wooler to Newcastle at 7.35pm on Sundays. Mrs.Hall was on the bus. As usual it had a standing load. One of the D.Ps was seated. He got up from his seat, bowed, handed Mrs.Hall the seat and said, very politely, 'kindly place your arse on the seat'! The bus erupted.

But to continue about bus services. The Edinburgh-Berwick-Newcastle service was restored to an hourly service in June 1946. After I was demobbed and back to Berwick we went shopping in Newcastle. With an employees' bus pass it had to be by bus, never mind the three-hour journey. Getting on at Berwick at 7.46am was no problem. Coming back from the Haymarket was. There were buses at 6.5pm, 7.5pm and 8.5pm, with duplicates on the 6.5 and 8.5. You had to be in the queue half an hour before departure to be sure of getting on. Summer was bad. There were lots of passengers through from Newcastle to Edinburgh. If you lived in Gosforth or Seaton Burn, don't even bother to go for a Berwick or Edinburgh bus - you won't get on. With luck you might manage it at Morpeth, otherwise go back into Newcastle for the bus. Seeing almost empty buses nowadays, you may think it hard to believe.

The SMT were quick to restore or introduce services. They stationed a bus at Duns, which they used, with help from Berwick, to run a new service to Bankend, Abbey St.Bathans, from early 1946, and others to Cranshaws, Longformacus and Heughhead Smithy later that year. A new Saturday and Sunday route, Service 279, ran between Berwick and Edinburgh via Greenlaw, Westruther and Lauder, worked by crews from both ends.

Needless to say we had no television so the cinemas were busy as were evening buses. This was particularly so on Saturdays when the country folk came in to go to the pictures.

United were under pressure to provide better facilities for these people and 1946 saw buses in places never seen before. There was a Saturday service to Pressen; that to Chatton was restored; some Norham buses were extended to Old Heaton; another ran between Belford and Elwick. A 1954 introduction by Mrs.Law, of Coldstream, was a circular service from Mindrum to Coldstream on Tuesday evenings for the cinema. The SMT ran another cinema service from Wark and Carham to Kelso on Thursdays.

In Berwick, itself, the 'prefabs' had been built at Valley View to ease the housing shortage. Despite their reputation at the time that ' you could lie in bed, put your hand up the chimney and open the front door', they were better that many had in the town. They created the need for a bus service. In October 1946 some journeys were put on to Quarry Corner. Building at Prior Park was under way by then. It needed a proper service; the Quarry Corner service was withdrawn, and a new route, Service 67B, from the Bus Station to Etal Way was introduced, soon running every 20-30 minutes.

Mention of Etal Way brings to mind other incidents. In that area lived Queenie who had a riding school - and was a regular passenger. One morning she boarded the first Etal Way bus at 7.10am, the only passenger. When the conductress came for her fare she said she had no money and offered an egg for the fare. The conductress viewed her riding whip with some trepidation and decided to take the egg. Queenie said, 'that egg is worth 3d, the fare is only 2½d, I want ½d change!' Stories about her are legion. Another former conductress told me, 'Queenie, oh, we had some incidents with her.' 'She used to bring buckets of corn on my bus to feed the horses'. 'Some of the conductors wouldn't let her bring the buckets on, I would.' She added, 'mind, she never brought the horse on the bus!'

Nothing to do with buses, this one concerns trains. One of the porters at Berwick Station was George Short, very smart, very military and very polite and helpful. This day Queenie rode up to

Yes, there were 'Sausage Queues' during the war. This queue formed a social club arranging day trips and social activities after the war. Mrs Tait, in the centre of this 1950s photo, was the organiser. Others include Miss Wallace, Mrs Hastings and Marion, Fisackerleys and the author's mother.

Berwick Station on horseback. Seeing George there she said, 'can you hold my horse for a moment, I just want to make an enquiry'. 'Certainly.' Queenie boarded a train to Edinburgh, leaving George holding the horse.

But back to more mundane things. There were not many schoolchildren travelling then, nothing to compare with today. Grammar schools attracted some scholars but the country schools were open. Fares remained at pre-war levels. Berwick-Newcastle was 5/2d single, 9/- return (26p, 45p); Edinburgh was 4/10d and 8/6d. Spittalers could buy a 12-journey ticket between Spittal and Berwick for 1/6d, which had to be bought at the Bus Station. Workers went home midday for their dinner then.

Bus traffic continued to flourish, peaking in 1954. To illustrate how it had developed, these are some figures from United.

In 1938 United had 891 buses running 38 million miles, carrying 117 million passengers and employing 3700 staff. In 1954 they had 1051 buses running 46 million miles, carrying 201 million passengers and employing 5450 staff. By 1985 those 201 million passengers had fallen to 86 million.

United and SMT provided many jobs locally, employing nearly 150 staff in Berwick.

Wartime and post-war produced difficult conditions for the engineering staff. New buses were rationed and spares were difficult as the motor works were turned over to munitions. Staff had to do, and did, the best they could. Old buses long due for scrap had to be retained. When I started in Berwick in March 1949 there was still a Bristol B type, B 17, in service. It had to be the last to go out in service, and not very far at that. It went at the end of that summer. Other elderly petrol AECs, AR 8, 13, 14, 15, remained in service for some time after that. They, too, were kept on local services only running to Newcastle as duplicates when they had to go to Jesmond Works for docking.

At the peak time in 1954, Berwick's United depot had 17 buses allocated; Wooler had 11; Berwick SMT had 20, all single-deckers. Double-deckers would come later. Many older buses were fitted with new bodies. To put the engineering work in perspective, I examined official records of United, now housed in Durham Record Office. They record that by 1947 a vast number of United buses had exceeded 500,000 miles. Those running the biggest mileages were the LDO type, Leyland Titan TD1 double-deckers, new in 1929-30. In their seventeen-year life, many had run more than 1,000,000 miles, averaging almost 60,000 miles each year.

The LDO type deckers never ran in Berwick but some of the Berwick vehicles did big mileages. A Leyland Tiger TS7, AHN 385, fleet no. LTO 6, new in 1935, had run 600,000 miles by 1947, an annual average of 50,000 miles. It was later given a new body, surviving until 1954. Just balance this against today's vehicles.

THE END OF THE HONEYMOON

The boom days of 1954 would never return. Wartime austerity had ended, petrol was available, and cars were available. Television was coming into vogue, cinemas were going out, with them the picture queues, the evening bus passengers and, in time, the services themselves. Fares were increased. The two factors which had kept bus usage high - wartime austerity and low fares - were no longer there and the downward spiral began.

Before Hitler's War some buses were one man operated but most had conductors, even the 14 seaters crossing Berwick's Old Bridge. Both United and SMT were fully crew operated on services around Berwick during and after the War. Economies had to be made and one manning was seen as the answer.

Now I have no intention of being politically correct and calling it 'one person operation'. I had little to do with one manning in United but much to do in Stockport. In the latter we employed women drivers. They had to do the same work as the men; they were paid the same as the men; they went 'one manning' when their turn came. No apologies for using the term.

United converted a few single-deckers to try to make them suitable for such use on rural services. They went in first at Ripon, then Carlisle and in 1958 at Alnwick. OMO did not come to Berwick until 1965. SMT started later. They had a little one manning in the Border area from 1969 but bigger conversions did not come until the 1970s. Both companies had to face personal problems with staff who could not transfer either on health grounds, age, or inability to learn to drive. Many staff at all the depots had been employed for years and could not adapt to another system at their age. Eventually all buses became one manned as the last of the old hands retired.

Not all was doom and gloom. Some new facilities were necessary. Pringle of Scotland had their new factory on the Ord Road Trading Estate in Tweedmouth, as did others, so they had to be served in the 1960s. More Council houses were built at Spittal Hall and they got a few journeys in 1965. My mother lived high up off Spittal Hall Road. She didn't live to see the bus service started, having to use the Spittal bus and an uphill walk to get home from Berwick. Her usual request to the conductor was, 'Wuthering Heights, son.' She was never asked where she meant. In time the Spittal Hall service would be much increased and extended to Highcliffe.

By the mid 1960s all the extensions, etc., introduced post-war i.e. to Pressen, Old Heaton, Edinburgh via Westruther et al were withdrawn but other major factors came into play. Education changed; local schools were closed; schooling was to be split into Primary, Middle and High Schools, with the latter two concentrated in Berwick, Wooler and Alnwick. So the demand for schools transport increased dramatically. It was no longer feasible to use Patten's taxi to bring a few scholars from Milfield and Ford to Berwick; they were coming in droves and double-deckers were necessary.

SMT began to run double-deckers between Berwick and St Abbs; United brought deckers to Berwick, at first, lowbridge Bristols. Three highbridge Bristols were allocated in 1968 to work on Spittal and Prior Park, remaining until 1970. None of these was suitable for one manning. As time went by, school buses became the peak traffic with both Berwick and Wooler having a double-deck allocation, mainly Bristol VRs. The nature of buses had changed totally, most having either underfloor or rear engines. There are books for anyone who wants more detailed information about the buses of the period.

In 1950 a new bus operator emerged in Berwick. Ralph Swan, who had joined United in 1934 when John Young sold out, bought a Commer coach, ENL 690. His was a wholly private hire operation, successful enough to buy another coach soon after. Ralph carried on with private hires, later obtaining school contracts.

SMT Berwick drivers c.1953. From the left: Willie Short, Bert Anderson, DTS J.Todd, Harry Hudson, Tom Slater, Jack Williams, Bob Colven, Jackie Hay, Tom Crombie, Jock Lauder and Fred Voase.

After bus de-regulation in 1986, he took over most of the former United and SMT services between Berwick and Norham and Berwick and Kelso via Cornhill which his son still runs, also using double-deckers.

Walkers of Wooler and E.R.Laidler also moved into the contract market for Wooler schools.

The one highlight of the 1970s was the introduction of the bus service to Holy Island in 1972. Traditionally the Island had been served by old taxis which rusted quickly from the salt water. Old-fashioned horse brakes were still being used up to wartime. A causeway was built in 1954 for part of the crossing. Only when the bridge over the River Low was opened was the bus service possible. It was not totally trouble-free. I believe one bus got stuck in the sand and stood there overnight. It is the only scheduled bus service to run to a TIDE table. George Daniels, at United's Gallowgate office, prepared the annual timetable. 'Lulu' Kyle kept a watchful eye on the Island end of the service. It was busy enough to need deckers; indeed one of the annual pilgrimages to the Island needed fifteen deckers to accompany the walkers.

An interesting innovation on the other side of the Border in 1979 was the 'Border Courier'. This was a joint effort by the Borders Regional Council, the Local Health Authority, the Scottish Development Agency and the Scottish Bus Group whereby five routes were provided, some from the Eastern Borders, to and from Peel Hospital carrying passengers, medicines, stores, etc. SMT ran it at the start. Peel Hospital closed when the new Borders General Hospital opened at Melrose. Since 1979 the 'Courier has been run partly by private operators as well as the SMT. Its routes have been revised but its purpose remains. Purpose built buses are used to ensure segregation of passengers and goods. It is a model of good scheduling providing, as it does, a variety of facilities for schools and works as well as the Hospital.

In more recent times we have seen the town bus services extended. The Pastures, Robert's Lodge and the West End all got services. The latter had had a long wait - they had wanted one in the 1930s. Wooler, too, got its local buses to take residents up the hill to High Fair and from Weetwood Avenue. Not bad for a place the size of Wooler!

I wonder where we go from here?

Ralph Swan stands on the step of the Commer Avenger with which he set up in business in 1950. His private hire was visiting Norham Castle.

J.Walker started his business from his Glendale Garage, Station Road, Wooler in 1946 with two Thornycroft Handy 20-seaters. This one, JR 4284, on the car park at Morden Street, Newcastle, was bought from R.Tait, Knowesgate. Walker ceased running in 1971. *(R.C.Davis)*

The first service bus to Holy Island, United's Bristol Lodekka MHN 525E stands there in 1972.

The classic Holy Island view. Bristol VRT YHN 655M on the bridge over the River Low. This is where unwise motorists become stranded trying to beat the tide. *(United)*

25. WORKING CONDITIONS ON THE BUSES IN THE 1950s AND BEFORE

Working conditions are such a big subject that I can only just touch upon them here. Luckily I had kept a 'Memorandum of Agreements (1946-1949)' between United , the Transport & General Workers Union and the National Union of Railwaymen. It is easy to establish conditions from that. SMT would have had comparable agreements.

But, moving back long before that we know little or nothing about conditions. When the buses were in the hands of small operators they were often worked by family members. Other employees had to get on and do what they were told to do. There were no regulations limiting drivers' hours on grounds of safety - they would come later. Pay - well you took what you could get. One local farm worker who could drive buses used to get somebody else to do his farm work on a Saturday - and pay him 1/- per hour, the going rate. He, himself, then went to United and did bus driving for 1/4d per hour. When Thompson, Young and Spowart were bought out, some staff came to United as casual staff only. They got bus driving only when required and that might mean driving the Newcastle-London service. At other times, and with no work at United, they had to take whatever other casual work they could find. Those who decried Trades Unions do not know how necessary their existence was.

United were reluctant to recognise Unions and their agreement to recognise both T&G and NUR did not come until 1935-36. The oddity is the appearance of the NUR. This arose because some employees were members of the NUR having been employed by the LNE Railway and whose services were taken over by United. There were no 'closed shops' so membership was voluntary. Union membership was always a contentious item. SMT had a strike in 1912 over dismissals. Some of their staff had joined a Union, becoming active participants, and were dismissed for that reason.

Returning to United's 1936 Agreement the hourly rates were: - drivers, 1/4d; conductors, 1/0½d; conductresses, 11¼d. Cleaners were paid 1/- for day work, 1/1d for nights.

Until 1939 drivers had to carry a tool kit and were responsible for breakdowns on the road.

Discipline was meted out if drivers had delays. Petrol averages were kept for every bus and league tables exhibited. That made for widespread abuse, either by siphoning from other buses, or, what I was told. Buses had to be filled at the end of the day. Given that they had been to Newcastle or Edinburgh they needed a lot of fuel. Certain drivers did not fill their bus 'up to the top', giving a favourable mpg for that day. The next driver needed more petrol than average and faced discipline.

Between 1939 and 1947 wage rates increased and, 'Conductors' maximum rates have advanced from amounts ranging between 36/- and 64/- for a 48 hour week to 101/6d for a 44 hour week. 'Drivers' rates had risen from 60/- to 105/6d.

Wages and conditions for those who worked on the Corporation buses were much better than those on companies like United. At Berwick the differentials were not so apparent but it was very important at Newcastle, for example, where they were. The Unions had always sought parity or near with the municipal men by virtue of a 'National Conditions Agreement'. The 'Gorman' Enquiry in 1947 gave a step towards that but full parity was never achieved. This would have dire effects later in places like Coventry where the motor industry attracted workers. Coventry City Transport had better pay and conditions than Midland Red, and the consequences must be obvious.

So in 1947 United staff had a 6-day, 44 hour working week; a daily guarantee of 7 hours pay; increased overtime pay and additional paid holidays. In time would follow the 11-day fortnight then the 5-day week.

Because of the shift work penalty payments i.e. for working on Sundays, for spreadover duties (in excess of c.10 hours start to finish), overtime, etc., were the norm in the industry. The weekly rate for 44, or whatever, hours was broken into an hourly rate, expressed in three decimal places. For example a weekly rate of 97/6d paid an hourly rate of 2/2.591d. For pay purposes working time was calculated down to twelfths of an hour. Annual holidays after three years continuous service were 10 days with 73 hours pay. But you might not last out the three years. Berwick depot needed more staff in summer than in winter so staff might have to leave at the end of the season or transfer to another depot, Ashington, Blyth or Whitley Bay, until a vacancy arose again at Berwick.

As office staff we had to calculate the time sheets weekly. The working week finished on a Saturday evening, quite a lot of overtime was worked, and the time sheets had to be completed, authorised, and sent to Newcastle on the 12.45pm bus on Sunday. They went on by bus to Darlington where money was put to hours for payment the following Friday.

A bit about the duties now. The timetable for a given service is prepared, agreed, etc., after which it is broken down into work for each individual bus and set out on a 'running time card'. On the United, buses were not buses, but 'cars'. Spittal-Highfields needed three buses - United had the 'A' and 'C' cars, SMT had the third. From these so-called bus workings daily duties were devised by the Schedules Dept. in Darlington. They had to be within the law on Drivers' Hours and to have the agreement of the Union representatives. There were 'good' and 'bad' duties in the eyes of the staff. One late duty took over the 'A' car on Spittal at 4.3pm, working it until 7.48pm. It then took a break and went elsewhere. That bus got everything, schools, workers and picture goers. Crew duties on the United were arranged in alternate early and late weeks, giving a rota length of about 30 weeks. Drivers went 'down' the rota, duties 1,2,3, etc, while conductors went 'up' the rota. Thus drivers and conductors had a different mate for each week until they met again. SMT staff worked a different system. They worked as regular crews, some for years together. Their duties were prepared locally. SMT Edinburgh worked some of the Newcastle services. On that via Berwick they worked the 8.5am and 9.5am ex Edinburgh, 12-hour duties. Three crews worked on each, doing a trip to Newcastle every third day, with short duties on the other working days. They were all long service staff who worked them. One crew in my time were driver Willie Burt and conductor George Ward. Willie did not retire from working that road until he was seventy.

One feature common to both United and SMT was the 'changeover'. On Service 12, Newcastle-Berwick-Edinburgh, United buses worked from Jesmond, Morpeth, Alnwick and Berwick depots. A bus starting at one end did not necessarily finish at its original depot and crews

had to change buses en route to get themselves back home. For example, the 7.46am from Berwick finished at Morpeth at 11.15pm. Buses were sorted out by engineering staff and changed over on the next day. This was common practice on United and worked without major problem. Berwick staff had changeovers at Buckton, Brownieside, Newton on the Moor, Peacock Gap, etc. SMT had a similar arrangement. Willie Burt's bus, the 8.5am from Edinburgh returned there at 7.30pm to work the 8.5pm to Berwick, where it finished. Their Berwick staff had change overs at Macmerry and Niddrie Cross Roads.

Services 9,12 and 15 between Newcastle and Edinburgh were jointly operated. The agreement required that operating mileage be equated between the two companies. That was done by exchanging mileage. One bus working from Berwick did the 8.25am to Edinburgh, back to Newcastle, and then back to Berwick at 8.45pm. As it could be operated by either company from Berwick it was used to balance the mileage - sometimes with United, sometimes with SMT, but always for a full season.

United's conductors were controlled by the Local Traffic Superintendent, himself reporting to the Area Traffic Superintendent at Gallowgate, Newcastle. Engineering and cleaning staff worked for the Depot Foreman, Bill Huntly in my time. He was responsible to the Area Engineer, and never the twain should meet.

Buses allocated to both United and SMT were kept in immaculate condition and there were few breakdowns. That applied equally at depots other than Berwick. Philip Groves, well known in the bus industry, came to United in 1954. He had to visit the depots and told me, 'when I came to Berwick in the staff car, I was always made to park it in a given space and a rectangle of sawdust was put under it.' Ian Richardson, then the Late Shift Foreman, said that they marked parking bays with white paint and always had rectangles of sawdust under each sump. They kept the floor clean with caustic soda.

UNIFORMS AND OTHER MISFITS

The SMT staff were fitted out with dark blue uniforms, caps for the women, hard hats for the men. They were worn at all times - or else. The

An SMT institution retires. Driver Willie Burt, from New Street, was retiring from the Edinburgh - Newcastle run, aged 70. He worked the 240-mile round trip every third day. The SMT DTS, Jimmy Todd, made the presentation. From the left: Gordon Wilson, Evelyn Morton, George Ward, Tom Crombie, Jane Ann Dryden, Annie Weatherburn, Willie Burt, Mrs Fiddes, Dod Thompson, Isobel Moir, Jimmy Todd, Cond. Anderson, Bob Garland, Isobel Johnson, Norman Strassheim.
Berwick bus station, 1968.

Two immaculate busmen in the early 1930s. Jodhpurs and leather leggings were standard until 1936. Goods were carried on roof racks and conductors had to climb a ladder to reach them. Driver Fred Voase is on the left and the conductor is Bobby Flynn, from Berwick.

men had had to wear leather leggings until 1936. Their staff at Berwick and Kelso were well turned out, universally immaculate. United staff did not have the same quality uniforms. They had jackets, trousers and caps, the latter optional. In summer they had dustcoats, beige with red trimming. No matter how well they tried to keep their dustcoats washed and pressed and their machine belts polished, they could never come up to the SMT standard. One bit of equipment they did get was a 'quick change'. In that you could store your sixpences and shillings, for easy change giving. These coins, and the old three-penny pieces would otherwise get lost in the cash bag.

The male ticket clerks were given a dustcoat. Ours was a flecked dark grey with red trimming. Trying to buy standard uniform sizes for staff who are basically misshapes is always a problem, or very expensive. United did not expend money on fripperies. It seems that uniforms came in two sizes, too little and too big. Ticket Clerks' dustcoats did not have even that standard of luxury. They were designed to fit men of at least 6'3", with a 44" chest. With a few minor alterations they would do for anybody smaller. Mine was almost ankle length, getting in the way of everything and I could not abide it. I think it finished up doing what its name entails - covering furniture when we were decorating.

CASH - AND THE BANK

Ticket clerks had a variety of jobs. Ticket machines had to be refilled and ticket stocks controlled, waybills made up, parcels accepted, enquiries answered - and cash dealt with. United conductors, on completion of duty, had to count and bag their takings, put them in a canvas bag and drop them in a night safe in the office. Next morning, when both clerks were in, the safe was opened with two sets of keys, the bags taken out, the cash counted and balanced - and banked.

On Friday morning there was another job. The pay slips for all the depot staff were beamed in from Darlington payroll office. You had to 'coin' for the pay. That meant going through every individual payslip and calculate exactly how many pound notes, ten bob notes, shillings, pennies, etc. you would need. As you bagged up the conductors' takings you had to ensure you had the right number of coins organised as you had to take the takings to Barclays Bank, pay them in, then draw them out again for the payroll. You then carried them back to the office and made up the pay packets which must be ready for 12 noon. While you were doing this, Peter Weatherburn would arrive from Harry Taylor, the pork butcher, with miscellaneous parcels of sausage to go by specified buses. He was only one of many regulars.

But the bank - money was taken to Barclays in Hide Hill - precisely at 10.0am when it opened. Securicor had not been invented. You carried the cash down High Street in a very obvious brown

Securicor incognito? The bus, a United Bristol with Willowbrook body, is unusual, the location more so. The driver hasn't gone down Berwick High Street by mistake. The destination is to fool the public and the bus is going to Barclay's Bank. Harry Taylor's shop is on the right - the home of the 'Sausage Queue'. (Photobus)

leather portmanteau. Given that Spittal and Prior Park buses generated a lot of copper, you had a green canvas bag doing its best to slip out of the other hand with the weight it contained. Monday was the worst day. Two days' takings were there and Saturday was the busiest of the week. For pure vulnerability Friday could not be beaten. You came back up High Street with the contents of c.80 pay packets, some with extra holiday pay. How we ever escaped the eyes of Berwick's mafia of the day I do not know.

Anyway, I've got to the bank. Now banking in 1952 bore little resemblance to 1999. Bank accounts were not universal. Elderly ladies with bank accounts planned days in advance when they would visit the bank and donned their fur coats that day. At Till number one was the Chief Cashier, Arthur Cairns, a local institution. Arthur only dealt with elderly ladies in fur coats, honorary Aldermen and comparable noteworthies. United's ticket clerks were definitely 'non grata'. Only in dire emergency would we be permitted to discharge our load at Till 1. We had to move down to Tills 2 or 3 where we had the friendly faces of George Foster, Betty Bainbridge, Alan Armitage or sundry youths aspiring to reach Till 1 during their working lives.

In due course the cash became greater or my muscles weaker but we went to the bank by bus. The idea of double parking a United bus on Hide Hill outside Barclays may not have appealed to all but at least the Police said nothing.

If Arthur is standing at the counter of the Barclays Bank branch on high I wonder what he thinks of banking now. It's called 'armchair banking' but done away from an armchair. An anonymous female says, 'Good morning, welcome to the Co-operative Bank! Please enter your account number (14 digits) followed by a 'hash' - pause - 'your details have been verified, please press...' And having again pressed 'hash', another anonymous female announces at 10-second intervals, 'your customer advisor will be with shortly.' Having been bombarded with piped music you can't stand, eventually a human voice identifies you and you are there! It's not like the old days, 'come back, Arthur, all is forgiven!' That was only the United. The SMT had a similar performance sorting out their cash. I never asked Mrs.Fiddes how she fared.

As for the ticket clerks, Douglas Faill was there when I started but left soon after and spent the rest of his working days working for Stoddarts. He was a great salmon fisher and ghillie. He lived in Tweedmouth and lost many hats, blown off when going 'ower the bridge'. In Berwick you go 'ower' the bridge, not 'across' it. For most of the time the others were Jimmy Shanks and Lila Reveley. Jimmy had just come out of the KOSBs after twenty-two years. He had drilled recruits in the Barracks and it was said that he could, without ever leaving the Barracks, march them out, along the Parade and down Church Street, still shouting the orders! On the other hand Lila was a very quiet soul. There was another clerk in the depot. When I started it was Edna Weatherburn (Mrs.Short). She was followed by Margaret Sanderson (Mrs.Hardwick). They used to come and help us when we were busy. Margaret was a long time member of the Operatic Society. She came and practised the words of some of the choruses. I must have been word-perfect when they did 'Maritza' and 'The Lilac Domino.' We had also a parcel boy for deliveries as we did a roaring trade in parcels by bus. They never stayed long. Some were not too bad - others were totally donnert!

After I left to go to Newcastle, Ernie Collins and Jimmy Virtue transferred from driving. Jimmy had been a POW in Japan, both very nice chaps, with lovely handwriting. Looking back, my time at Berwick Bus Station had two sides; we were horribly badly paid; otherwise it was a happy one. Naturally we had our bad days, but we had a lot of laughs, too.

26. BERWICK BUS STATION

It is now just a memory. In its day it was described as 'a red blot on the town centre' amongst other things. Nikolaus Pevsner was not complimentary about it. 'Marygate has been sadly damaged in its unity and compactness by the street which leads into it from the new bridge, and by the bus station facing this.' Like it or no, it served its purpose.

I have already noted that buses had started from High Street and that they were garaged either at the A&B Garage in Silver Street or at Chisam's Garage in Castlegate. Silver Street could not have continued as a longer-term bus garage.

This is what the Bus Station replaced - the corner of Chapel Street and Walkergate. The property dated from c.1750 and would have been built of stone quarried from Berwick Castle. The rear of the United depot would occupy the site.

from the Council. At this time Highfields was being built and to where the tenants of Weatherley Square were being rehoused. That square lay behind High Street with access through arches, while another street, Narrow Lane, gave access from High Street to Chapel Street roughly along what is now the side of Woolworths. Pevsner was no doubt correct on his comments about losing the unity of Marygate. But Weatherley Square was a rabbit warren of slum property with access only to High Street. It was past refurbishment.

Plans were submitted in September 1936 for two garages each housing 20 buses. No doubt the purchase, jointly by SMT and United, went through without trouble. The SMT must have begun to use their garage in May/June 1937, using the rear entrance in

The first mention I have seen of a bus station is a proposal by United and SMT in 1931 'to build a Bus Station on land owned by the Borough on the east side of the North Road.' This cannot have been a bus station but a bus garage. A lot of argument brewed about buses blocking High Street. By 1933 there was pressure to build a bus station.

Early in 1935 the Council received a letter from SMT. The Company had agreed to purchase land from Albert Williams for a Bus Station and Garage, and they needed land also

Chapel Street, with an office inside the garage. 'Notices and Proceedings' of the Traffic Commissioners indicate that Spittal buses would use the Bus Station from late June 1937. It was not finished then as a newspaper reported in July 1937 that a painter had been injured while painting the roof.

It would be in full use by the end of the summer 1937. It received no publicity when it opened maybe because it did not have an official opening. It just seems to have happened. United did not terminate their agreement to use the

Berwick 1934. Turning from Golden Square into High Street is TY 4396, an Albion PK26, new to John Young in 1928, becoming CM93 in the United fleet. The scene would soon change. The block between the Berwick Advertiser and the Lion Garage, which fronted run-down property of Weatherley Square, would soon go to make room for the Bus Station - with one exception. The National Wallpaper Stores was leased and would remain *in situ* until after the war. *(Berwick Guild of Freemen)*

Berwick Bus Station in better days in October 1968. The enquiry offices are still in the centre; the footpath in the foreground is where the wallpaper shop stood. *(P.M.Battersby)*

A&B Garage until 20th October 1937.

Albert Williams had his shop, including the former SMT office, at 88, High Street. Next door, no. 86 was occupied by the National Wallpaper Company. Presumably it was on a lease and it had to be left standing. It was tidied up with the same bricks as the Bus Station, and on an island in the middle of the station frontage, created a separate entrance and exit. It stood there until after the War and, literally, disappeared one day, leaving the island. It remained like that for many years, the only other alteration being the removal of the two enquiry offices which stood in the centre.

An embarrassing incident for a mother one day. There were toilets across the station from the loading points. A small boy sped across from a queue and disappeared into the Gents. A few minutes later a piping voice broadcast to the waiting queues, 'Mam, there's nae paper!'

In recent years structural problems began to develop and the place showed an increasing aura of dereliction, doing nothing for the town's image. By February 1996 the garages had to be vacated, the buses being transferred to the MoT Testing Station on the Ord Road Trading Estate, but the bus services continued to use the rest of the Bus Station.

Early in 1998 some services were moved from the Bus Station to terminate at the Railway Station with a town centre stop in Golden Square. In August 1998 the garages were demolished and part of the site fenced off. There were long-term redevelopment problems.

In September 1998 buses were moved to a garage on the old A1 at Scremerston. A month later all bus stops were moved from the Bus Station site, most to 'Crawford's Alley.' That name was unlikely to enthuse the native Berwicker. As one of the latter but with a working life spent 'on the buses', I cannot recall a town centre main terminal quite so awful as that introduced in October 1998. Arrangements, even with the subsequent alterations, are a deterrent to usage and an encouragement to vandalise.

27. BUILT IN BERWICK

One might not expect to find the motor industry up here but Berwick had its own company building buses, the PICKERING MOTOR VEHICLE AND WHEEL CO. LTD.

In the first years of the century F.G.Pickering was advertising his 'Motor Car and Cycle Works' at Highgate, Tweedmouth, with a showroom at 80, Main Street, Tweedmouth. It seems he had put new equipment in these 'Highgate' Works and offered estimates for building any class of motor car or cycle as well as motor haulage wagons. I have not traced any Pickering-built cars.

Kelly's Directory for 1906 quotes the Pickering Motor Vehicle and Wheel Co.Ltd. which, *prima facie*, should have been registered under the Companies Acts. The Companies Registration Office has no record of this company so research is difficult or impossible.

What has come to light is that Pickering built a double-decker bus which was displayed at Cordingley's Show at the Agricultural Hall, Islington, in March 1906. This bus arrived late for the Show, the body coming first, then the chassis later, with the two married together just in time.

Pickering's double-deck omnibus exhibited at Cordingley's Show 1906 - built in Berwick.

The Show report in the 'Motor Traction' magazine of 5th April 1906 gives the specification, including a 35-40hp engine operating at 750rpm. It had two ignition systems, one the Eisemann magneto system, the other an accumulator, and coil ignition using separate sparking plugs. The wheels were a Pickering patent with a fixed centre flange; most of the engine control was located on the steering column, and it had a three-speed gearbox. The body, 'roomy and well finished', had 34 seats.

Pickering claimed to have an output of 300 vehicles - they do not say what the vehicles were - other than that 'they were kept fully engaged.'

One Pickering single-deck bus ran in Penrith at some time but the Show double-deck never ran. The Company ceased trading later in 1906.

So Pickering departed into oblivion and Berwick lost the chance of being another Leyland. The 'Motor Traction' report gives more technical information than appears above and it carries a picture of the double-decker, which cannot be reproduced clearly.

28. LONG DISTANCE COACH SERVICES

In recent years Berwick Borough has not been well served by these despite their popularity in other parts of the country. Years ago I went to Newcastle by bus to catch the overnight coach to London but it is not a journey I would take now. SMT Edinburgh-London coaches served the A697, only marginally convenient for people living en route. But it was not always thus.

The heyday of coaching was the late 1920s and the 1930s. The doyen of coach operators was ORANGE BROS., of Bedlington.

Brothers J. and R.Orange had been running buses around Bedlington since 1923. In June 1927 they had to return one of their Gilford coaches to its Holloway, London factory. They decided to try running it from Newcastle to London with a load of passengers. It was so successful they repeated the operation, and then ran twice a week until September 1927 when they began a daily service to London.

By taking only advance bookings they avoided the need to get licences from all towns en route.

In 1928 Orange Bros. opened a London office at King's Cross and began both day and night services. They became an associate of London Coastal Coaches, enabling them to use the new Victoria Coach Station where connections on from London were available. They moved their head office from Bedlington to the Haymarket, Newcastle, and built a new garage at Bedlington.

United and SMT had a through Newcastle-Edinburgh service from 1928. Orange Bros. were licensed to carry United/SMT passengers between Newcastle, Berwick and Edinburgh from March 1930 and, in September 1930, were permitted to extend their own London-Newcastle service to Berwick, Edinburgh and Glasgow. This time it was 'in conjunction with the LNE Railway', implying railway financial interest.

Orange Bros. timetable for Spring 1931 shows two daily journeys between London and Berwick. You could leave Victoria Coach Station at 11.0am, be at Berwick at 1.15am next day, or use the overnight service at 8.0pm, in Berwick at 10.55am, next day. Fares were 25/- single (£1.25) and 40/- return (£2.00). Buses were fitted with 'comfortable bucket seats' and passengers had pillows and travelling rugs. Fourteen of the buses had radios.

Railway financial interests would see an increasing involvement by United on their behalf. Orange Bros. fleet passed to United in August 1933, the brothers withdrew from the company and United became sole owners in April 1934. Such was their reputation that United kept the 'Orange Bros.' name for many years.

Orange Bros. started their service because they needed to get one of their Gilford buses to the factory. That was a normal routine for Gilford. Their buses were very successful around 1930 and it was their practice to bring customers' buses into their works for maintenance. Gilford's history is outside the scope of this book but I must mention the firm. They built quality and speedy coaches. They went bankrupt in the early 1930s partly because of the demise of their main customers, the private operators who were being taken over, and partly because they lost money developing a revolutionary double-decker, so far ahead of its time that it did not sell. It would not be equalled until the Bristol Lodekka appeared in the 1950s.

Orange Bros. did not have a monopoly on the London service. MAJESTIC COACHES owned by Armstrong, of Ebchester, ran, although not to Berwick. One of their London coaches, new in

1931, ended its days at Berwick reseated as a bus. It was AR8, UP 5434, withdrawn in 1950 and bought by the National Coal Board to carry miners to Scremerston Colliery.

Another London service operator was PHILLIPSON'S COACHES based in London. They were bought by United in 1934 and their buses transferred to the Orange Bros. fleet. Some of their AEC coaches, new in 1931, were reseated as buses, allocated to Wooler depot and survived until 1951/53 (ARO 24-27).

One London operator who did run to Berwick was GLENTON FRIARS, of Blaydon. Henry Brown and J.Glenton Friars ran buses from 1919. They had a London service running in 1928 which, when they were bought in 1932, had been extended from Newcastle to Berwick, Edinburgh and Glasgow. They offered fares comparable with the normal service buses north of Newcastle. The fare from Berwick to Glasgow was 8/1d single (41p), 13/6d return (68p). London was 41/6d return (£2.08p).

By 1931 eight companies ran between Newcastle and London, giving eighteen journeys daily, and more in summer.

Not all the long distance coaches were London bound. COUNTY MOTOR SERVICES had a Newcastle-Wooler-Kelso-Edinburgh-Glasgow service of which more in the chapter on Wooler and Glendale. The other was THOMAS ALLEN & SONS, Rink Street, Blyth. They ran a number of routes from Blyth to Newcastle, etc. In 1929 they began a daily service from Newcastle to Aberdeen via Wooler, Kelso, Edinburgh, Perth, Dundee and Montrose, advertising 'First Class Luxurious Saloon Coaches.' It lasted until 1934 when Allen sold out to United who withdrew the service.

EXCURSIONS AND TOURS

This is almost where we came in, as 'outings' were the starting point for many of the original operators. Turning back briefly to 1950, there were private operators like Ralph Swan carrying only private parties. They had to fulfil all the legal requirements relating to the construction and maintenance of their buses, but they did not need Road Service Licences. The latter were necessary only if regular bus services or excursions and tours advertised to the public were run.

SMT Berwick were getting new buses with seats more of a coach style. United concentrated on robust service buses without the frills. As a result SMT could offer day tours having licences for them. United had little in the way of licences. The only things running in my time were 'Mystery Tours' on a summer Sunday evening. They were hardly a mystery as only four destinations were authorised: - Bamburgh, Yetholm, Duns and one other. It was possible to fill a bus but what were used were the elderly Bristols normally running on Spittal or, later, some of the pre-war Leylands, which had received new bodies, still austere. Never mind, a trip to Yetholm was always worthwhile if you didn't have a car. It wasn't easily reached by service bus. Road Service Licences for tours were guarded jealously. United would never have got a licence for Kelso or Melrose. They did have one for the Roman Wall, which rarely ran, other destinations licensed included Beanley and Mindrummill. With respect to residents of Mindrum, I don't see it as a noteworthy destination.

Coaches were allocated to Berwick later, giving something suitable to duplicate the Newcastle-London service. Even before the War Berwick, in common with other depots, was called on to provide London 'dups', supplementing the regular London drivers who were based at Jesmond. Those duplicates did not need conductors but, because of the long journey times had to have two drivers per bus. Drivers had to lodge in London overnight - or over day if on the night service - staying in regular boarding houses near Victoria Coach Station, working back to Newcastle the next day or night. Good business for the boarding houses but a big draw on the depot's driving staff.

29. *MEMORIES*

How many times have I thought, 'what a fool I was for not noting down more of peoples' recollections.' There are still a few 'old hands' with good memories around so I asked some of them to tell me theirs. Some I have used in other parts of the text; this is a selection.

JAMES ELDER

He started as a conductor with Brook & Amos at

ESC 471, SMT B277 was a 1947 AEC Regal with Duple body from Kelso depot. It was photographed picking up a private party from Town Yetholm.

Galashiels in 1923, aged 16. He had a motorbike licence when, one day - he would be 18 - James Amos told him, 'take that bus to Bemersyde!' 'Where's Bemersyde?' Off he went. He started driving in earnest for the first Highland Show in Kelso in 1926. He was allocated an 18 seater Karrier charabanc (probably LS 1160, new in 1923). This was his own bus.

'Brakes on these buses were not the best', he said. 'I was sick of this bus; coming down the hill into Eyemouth from Coldingham one day, I shoved it out of gear.' 'It had poor brakes and the handbrake wasn't effective when the bus was empty.' 'The cable stretched tight when the bus was loaded, but this time it was slack and the brakes wouldn't work.' 'I landed in a burn at the bottom.' 'I had to pick up a party at Eyemouth to go to Whitley Bay, they were waiting for me in the Square.' 'There wasn't anybody I could ask so I went to Mrs.Blackie to see if her bus was available.' 'Luckily for me it was, and the party got away without too much delay.' Jimmy never told me what happened to the bus - or to him when James Amos found out.

However, back to the Karrier charabanc. 'It didn't have detachable wheels, the tyres were fitted to the rim.' 'I had only two punctures; after changing a tyre, it had to be pumped up to pressure from the engine.'

'I worked duplicates to the service buses and also summer tours.' 'St.Mary's Loch and Moffat were common destinations.' 'We caused a sensation when we passed through some villages where charabancs weren't usually seen', he said. The Karrier had a canvas hood. 'It was a job to erect it.' 'People insisted on helping and it got jammed, so I used to tell them, 'if it rains, I'll put the hood up, don't help me!'

About Brook & Amos, Jimmy said, 'there had been four Amos brothers, Andrew, James, Willie and Tom.' 'They came from Yarrow.' 'Tom was drowned; Andrew had a joinery business and did some bus work for them.' 'Brook & Amos bought out other operators, one of them had old chain-driven Caledons; I never drove them.' 'They were so noisy that the conductors couldn't hear what the back seat passengers were saying.' 'One of their buses was called 'Old Sheila'; as far as I know it was called after somebody in Darnick.' 'By 1928, mechanical changes made big improvements to the buses.'

Jimmy Elder was sent to Coldingham in 1927 to open up the Coldingham-Berwick service bought from Henderson. He, and his first conductor, fifteen-year-old Fred Voase, worked from the little garage in Fisher's Brae. He returned to Selkirk for a time, and then came to Berwick when SMT opened up there, working from Boston's Yard and, later, the A&B Garage.

'We worked two shifts; one at 8.45am from Berwick to Newcastle, back to Edinburgh and back to Berwick.' 'The other worked the 7.10am Berwick to Edinburgh, to Newcastle, back to Niddrie Cross Roads on the outskirts of Edinburgh, where we changed over with an Edinburgh crew, then back to Berwick at 10.45pm.' 'We were paid £2.15.0d per week (£2.75). (The 1930 Road Traffic Act introduced limits on drivers' hours. From what Jimmy Elder told me it seems they were not always observed)

Except for war service, Jimmy was a driver at Berwick until 1948, becoming District Superintendent on John Craig's retirement. He moved to Edinburgh in 1953 as Chief Inspector and then District Superintendent. He died in November 1999.

D.L.G.Hunter, in his book, 'From SMT to Eastern Scottish', notes that Gala Motor Co. had two Caledons, which were scrapped when SMT took over Brook & Amos. 'Old Sheila', he writes, was Brook & Amos fleet no. 6, always working the Galashiels-Melrose service.

GORDON WILSON

He is the man with the prolific memory. He has recounted so much to me over so many years. Many bits and pieces have been been used throughout the text, indeed, only the need to perpetuate what he told me motivated me to put pen to paper. The fact that his recollections are brief here reflects their use elsewhere in the book.

Gordon started his working life in Dodds, the grocers, in Berwick's High Street, becoming United's first conductor recruited at Berwick when they opened up there in 1928. He told me much about Amos, Proud and their staff who came to Berwick. About Watson Curry, a driver, he said, 'he was the archetypal busman'. 'He had a stomach ulcer and couldn't always eat his 'piece' at Edinburgh.' 'He used to get out the Brasso and polish the bus.' (ulcers were a common illness then and for many years later given that staff had irregular meals). Amos, Proud's men had dark green uniforms and, like

most bus drivers, wore leather leggings. 'United gave a full uniform, supplied by Manclarks of Edinburgh, in a grey material with red piping.' 'We were asked if we were in the Salvation Army!' 'The drivers didn't get the full outfit so Watson Curry went to Manclarks and bought one himself.'

'The Old Bridge was still in use when they came to Berwick.' 'They used full size buses, Leyland Lions or Tigers, going up and down Hide Hill and along Bridge Street.' 'One driver used to use West Street.' (For anyone unfamiliar with Berwick, West Street is a very steep, cobbled hill, just wide enough to take a bus).

Between 1928 and 1934 United staff worked only Newcastle or Edinburgh. 'The first buses allocated to Berwick were Associated Daimlers, United J type.' 'They had a galley at the back from which we had to serve tea, coffee and sandwiches.' 'Leaving Berwick we had to light a small paraffin stove to get boiling water - it would be ready by the time we got to Belford.' 'We had to ask the passengers if they wanted any of these and had to wait for them to eat and drink before we went on.' 'It wasn't popular with short riders who had to wait.' 'We got the sandwiches from Carricks in Northumberland Street in Newcastle.' 'We got a supply there to use en route to Berwick, taking back any unsold the next day.' 'We had to do this in our break time in Newcastle and the sandwiches had to be accounted for on our waybills.' 'It lasted only one season.'

Now Berwick has its own dialect; neither Northumbrian as spoken in Wooler, nor Lowland Scots as spoken in Eyemouth. 'Geordies' say we are Scots; Scots say we aren't. About working to Newcastle and Edinburgh, Gordon said, 'we were bi-lingual.' 'We had to take our own sandwiches; if it was Newcastle, we took our 'bait'; if it was Edinburgh, we took our 'piece.' 'Some passengers would try to mislead us by asking for a stop and using a strange name.' 'There were three different names for Bilsdean Road End - we got wise to it.'

In 1934 the three local operators, Spowart, Thompson and Young were taken over.

'It was the Saturday of the March Hirings, one of the busiest days of the year.' 'John Young had been made Traffic Superintendent by United'. 'He gave one of his drivers a double shift on Newcastle and Edinburgh - he had never worked those before. He gave me a double shift on the Low Road to Spittal, with no break at all.' 'I asked JY, what about a break?' 'He said, just get yourself a pie and a bottle of lemonade, you'll be alright!'(15 hours without a break and totally illegal).

Gordon was working on the Low Road to Spittal. A car was parked in Bridge Street and shop blinds were down opposite. He could not get past. The Police Inspector was on his bus. 'Wait there, I'll soon get it shifted!' Gordon said, 'when he eventually came back he told me, 'that car belonged to the Vicar of Spittal, I couldn't say too much to him!'

A remarkable co-incidence he related was this. The two conductors who started with him in 1928 were twin brothers, Jack and Jim Robson who spent their working lives with United. Now I must say that Berwick's buses rarely had mechanical breakdowns. This day one Robson signed on duty and went off to Edinburgh; the other went later to Newcastle. Then a telephone call

Photographed after a presentation for 40 years service. From the left: Bob Garland, twins Jim and Jack Robson, Gordon Wilson. Berwick depot 1969.

The smiling pair advertising SMT excursions and tours from Berwick are Tom Slater and Jimmy Elder. Circa 1952.

came, 'this is Jack Robson, I'm on Newcastle but I've broken down at Beal.' Not long after, another call, 'this is Jim Robson, I'm on Edinburgh, I've broken down at Biel Gates.' To get two breakdowns together was unusual. To get two breakdowns involving twin brothers at places with virtually the same name was remarkable.

Gordon became Local Traffic Superintendent when John Young resigned in 1946, retiring in 1973 when Jack Robson succeeded him.

Another well-known United figure was BOB GARLAND, an Inspector when I started. A tall, slim man, he had a long nose. He often told this against himself. He was walking home during the blackout. There were big gates at the back of his house. In the blackness he had his arms outstretched to find the gates when he got such a smack on his nose. His hands had gone through the gaps in the gates. 'I knew I had a long nose but I never knew it was longer than my arms.' We had many laughs with Bob, now long since gone.

BERWICK'S LONGEST SERVING BUSMAN

It must be TOM SLATER. He started as a conductor with the SMT in 1936. After military service he returned to SMT as a driver. He told the 'Berwick Advertiser', 'we used to have to wear breeches and leggings years ago because the buses were colder and we had separate cabs.' He was one of the first one-man drivers at SMT Berwick, from which he retired in 1984. Tom didn't take happily to retirement so he went to work part-time with Swan's buses, whose depot was just around the corner from his house. They had most of the Berwick-Norham-Kelso service plus several school contracts. Tom continued with them until eventually retiring in April 1999 after 63 years service. Bear in mind that bus drivers are subject to a thorough medical annually - and you have to be fit to pass it!

EDDIE UNWIN

Eddie recorded two tapes for me. They give an enlightening picture of working conditions in the 1930s.

He started as a cleaner on the railway but was paid off aged 16. No redundancy pay then, you finished and that was that. After 18 months unemployment he started on the United as a conductor just before his 18th birthday in 1930. At Berwick were four drivers, Bill Cossar, Tommy Miller, Ninian Kinross and Watson Curry, and four conductors, Gordon Wilson, Jack and Jim Robson and Eddie.

'There were two buses and four shifts, either Edinburgh or Newcastle.' 'We had to work seven days a week.' (despite the Road Traffic Act!) 'One late shift left Edinburgh at 9.30pm and you had to clean the bus on arrival at Berwick.' 'The driver cleaned the bodywork; the conductor cleaned the windows and was issued with a small sweeping brush to clean the interior.'

'Training, oh, you just went on the bus with the senior conductor, Gordon Wilson, he taught you.' 'We had rack tickets, the ticket boxes went to Alnwick for checking.' 'When the office opened in West Street we had two ticket clerks, Billy Inglis and Arthur Morrison.' 'You paid your money into them and read off the ticket numbers to the clerk, who checked them.'

'In those days it was a job.' said Eddie. 'Pay was 18/6d a week during training, 22/6d after that.' 'It wasn't well paid, you survived.'

United bought up local operators in Wooler; Gray, Hilton, etc. Eddie was sent from Berwick to Wooler. 'You had to go to Wooler or you had no job.' 'You didn't want to be on the dole, it was a stigma then.' 'I had to go into digs at Wooler; they cost £1.00 a week; I earned 22/6d and got pocket money from my mother.' He recalled working as conductor on a charabanc acquired with T.R.Gray's business. He had to take the fares from the running board of the moving charabanc.

A Bristol B-type was later allocated to Wooler, garaged at Walker's Garage, Station Road, now South Road. County Motors garage was opposite the United. Arthur MacLean, the ex-Pile driver, was then United's mechanic. 'Buses were hard to start in winter so Arthur devised a method.' 'He took some waste material on to open ground, lit a small fire, withdrew the sparking plugs from his bus and heated them in the fire.' 'They kept a long handle which they pushed on to the starting handle, he pulled, I kicked until it started.' 'Once warmed it started easily.' 'County did not do this and often came to Arthur for a tow - which they got.' 'I don't know what United management would have done had they known we were helping the competitors.'

There were two crews at Wooler. One of the conductors was sacked, so Eddie had to work double shifts. He was then sent to work at Alnwick, again having to pay digs, but did get sent back to Berwick.

United bought County Motors Newcastle-Wooler-Edinburgh service in 1933, taking it over about 23rd April 1933. Two United crews were sent from Berwick to Kelso to work a United bus to be garaged there, drivers Tommy Miller and Ninian Kinross; conductors Jack Robson and Eddie. On the Saturday before take-over, Ninian and Eddie were sent passenger to Newcastle where they boarded the last County service to Wooler at 8.0pm. On arrival at Wooler, the County crew left the bus, leaving Ninian and Eddie to take it on in service to Kelso. It was parked in Croall, Bryson's garage near the end of Kelso Bridge. 'It was a narrow arch on a bend, tight to get a bus in.' 'We had a modern bus at Kelso. It had curtains at the windows, a retractable flap at the door and I think it had an experimental 5th gear.'

There were two duties for the two crews and again they had to work a seven day week. 'One duty started at 5.30am, you had to clean the bus, then work Kelso-Newcastle and back, finishing at 4.0pm.' 'The late shift took over at 4.0pm to Edinburgh and back to Coldstream, then to Kelso.'

Now United crews had travel passes, so had SMT, but each was available only on their own buses. 'It was OK for the drivers, they were married and they brought their wives to Kelso.' Jack Robson and Eddie were single and wanted to come home sometimes. 'We were prepared to pay the 1/4d fare from Kelso to Berwick, the same as the SMT staff paid, but we were refused. When we wanted to come home we had to pay the full 4/6d return, a high fare compared with that to Edinburgh.' Not only that, they had this 7-day week to work. 'We had to arrange between ourselves when we wanted to come home. The conductor who worked the late shift on Saturday did a double shift on Sunday, then came in for the early turn Monday - so we could get home alternate weekends.'

The bus was moved from Kelso to Swan's Garage at Cornhill. Eddie's sister lived at Learmouth, within cycling distance, so he lodged there. Two conductors were recruited locally, allowing Jack and Eddie to return to Berwick.

His next move was to Newcastle and the driving school for six weeks. Six conductors from various depots were in the school with the Instructor, Bruce Hall. Eddie had never driven. 'At first we were allowed to use only 1st and 2nd gears. Some days we had to go into Jesmond Depot, go down the pits and watch the fitters working. We were on a Bristol J type at Stannington when the half shaft snapped. They had semi-floating rear axles. We had to take the wheel off, withdraw the broken half shaft, send to Jesmond for another and fit it ourselves.' Near the end of training they had to work 8.0pm to 8.0am for night driving experience. 'After that we were tested. There were trams on the road at Jesmond; we had to be careful not to cross the tramlines. The trams had better acceleration than we had and their drivers could make it difficult for us.'

Having lodged in Newcastle with Sandy Mutch, the ex-Newcastle United goalkeeper, Eddie passed his test and returned to Berwick.

Stenhouse of Yetholm had been bought out and United had an out-station there, with a driver, a conductor and a driver/conductor who worked the others rest days. On Saturdays the driver/conductor travelled to Berwick to work as a spare driver there.

Jack Robson, senior to Eddie, preceded him into the driving school and was then sent to Yetholm as driver/conductor. Eddie, having passed his test, was the junior. He was sent to Yetholm and Jack returned to Berwick. So Eddie was the driver/conductor, Sid Lunn was the driver and Jimmy Todd, ex John Young, Norham, was the conductor. (There are two Jimmy Todds. The other is SMT). United Jimmy Todd was a big, burly man and excitable. Jimmy Todd and Eddie were cleaning the bus, LT4-10, and Eddie couldn't get it to start. Jimmy Todd came across, 'oot o' ma way, ah'll show ye how tae start it!' 'He got the starting handle and, instead of clicking it up, decided to show his brute strength and began to swing it. It kicked back. How it didn't take his head off I'll never know, but it caught his glasses and sent them flying across the garage.'

In September 1939 Eddie went into the Fire Service and then the RAF. On his return in 1946 he worked first for Crown Coaches, from Washington, Co.Durham. He was based at

Easter Monday 1926 at Town Yetholm. John Turnbull of Kelso owned this Maudslay charabanc, Y7019. It had been new in May 1920 to Weston Motor Company, Weston-super-Mare (Robert Warrilow and Guy Moon). Turnbull bought it in Spetember 1920. The fashions and the buses have changed, the place has not.

Not strictly in the Berwick area, this Fiat 14-seater was owned by Dave Welsh and ran between Morebattle and Kelso in the 1920s. It was called *Lily of the Valley*. On the left is the owner, Dave Welsh; on the right, wearing leather leggings, is Jim Welsh.

Wooler, taking the P.O.Ws from the camp there out to work on the farms. By that time the prisoners, mainly German, were not under armed guard. When the camp at Weetwood Avenue closed he went to the Crown Coaches depot at Birtley. 'Digs were hard to get, I stayed in the Bevan Boys Hostel at Pelton Fell.' He returned to Berwick, worked one summer with the SMT before coming back to United until his retirement in 1978.

Eddie recounted various incidents. 'I was working on Service 61, coming from Spittal over the Old Bridge. Hardy's, the furnishers, had a shop in Hide Hill and big vans delivered there. I was returning from Spittal and was right at the top of the Old Bridge when a Hardy's lorry appeared. The boy assisting with the lorry got out to help guide the vehicles past each other. There is a big camber there and I was watching the mirror. I thought the vehicles must be touching - they were. The traffic was blocked, the Police came, and so did Bill Huntly, the depot foreman. He brought jacks from the garage to lift and release the vehicles. The boy said he was watching the tops of the vehicles and didn't see them get jammed. I thought I might be prosecuted, but I wasn't.'

On parcels traffic, Eddie said, 'the buses carried a lot of parcels, maybe 40 or 50, of various sizes. When we were on Service 15, farmers would bring eggs in long boxes down to the road end to go by bus. Maybe four or six seats would be taken up with parcels; all had to be entered on a sheet and signed over. Once I was given a calf in a sack.' When the office was in West Street we had to collect the parcels from there. The bus stops were in High Street. Every time the Playhouse and the Theatre changed their programmes the films had to be sent in big boxes to Newcastle by bus. They were very heavy. Either we had to carry them from the office or the bus would reverse down West Street for them.'

I asked Eddie if he had problems with the snow. 'I was going to Edinburgh with Tommy Miller on a Sunday at 8.30am when we ran into a drift at Cairncross. I got a lift to Reston from a garage owner whose car had chains fitted. I phoned for instructions and was told, 'go back and dig yourselves clear, turn back at Heughhead Smithy, go back to Ayton and wait time there. I had to walk a mile back to the bus and do that

regardless of the fact that we were soaking wet.' He was scathing in his comment, 'cattle were treated better!'

IAN RICHARDSON

Ian was an engineer with United, becoming late shift Foreman at Berwick, later working for Swan's buses, from which he retired in 1992.

He was on duty one night at United when a farmer came to him, 'whae wiz that on the last Norham bus? Ian checked the rota and told him. 'Here's a bag of baigies for him. Tell him next time he wants some tae ask me an' no help himsel' frae the field!.'

Baigies seemed to feature large in everyday bus life. A conductress told me about some of the perks from the country. 'We got eggs sometimes and, oh yes, we got baigies. I had a load of baigies for the staff rolling about my bus.'

For the uninitiated, baigies are swede turnips.

What Ian did tell me was about his father, John Richardson, also an engineer with United. John had served his time - five years - with the A&B Garage. He was then finished and went to work as an 'improver' at Redfearn's Garage in Golden Square, Berwick. They ran a couple of buses. John then got a job with Thompsons of Scremerston in 1923 as their first driver.

In 1934 Thompson sold out to United. John Richardson went to United - but only as a casual driver - and did not get full-time employment with them until 1939. 'He had to take whatever work they offered, and was only paid for what he did. He had to do whatever other casual work he could get. Sometimes he would have to do a Newcastle-London trip at short notice for which he got 19/- (95p) for the return journey.'

John stayed with the United during the War except for a period when he, and a bus, were requisitioned by the Army.

He was another very quiet man with a sense of humour. One of the engineering staff was known for 'hanging on' to any coins dropped on the bus floors. John decided to fool him. He nailed a coin to the wood frame of a seat. Somebody lost their fingernails trying to retrieve it.

Bus crews did not always look upon ticket inspectors with favour. Some were positively disliked. One United crew were working on Edinburgh where an unpopular inspector

SMT provided buses to take guests to the wedding of Lord Bruce and Miss Archer in 1959. The conductresses came from various depots and are pictured in Holyrood Park, Edinburgh. Cissie Burgon, from Berwick, is in the centre of the back row.

worked. With the conductor was a trainee. As the bus approached the stop the conductor said to his trainee, 'watch this.' As the Inspector boarded the conductor had a fit of coughing. The Inspector left the bus at the next stop.

Another Inspector story, this one concerning Charlie Brown, from Wooler. I have heard it more than once, but I can't vouch for its truth!

At the time Charlie was a driver and was working with a mate on the London service. They stopped at Leeming Bar, the refreshment stop, and not a place where passengers normally boarded. Two ladies came to board with luggage. Charlie told them, 'just leave it there', and went off to join his mate for tea. When the two drivers returned to the bus, Charlie took the ladies' luggage and climbed on to the roof to stow it but without telling his mate who got into the cab and drove off. Charlie was stranded on the roof of the moving bus. He could not attract the driver's attention so he crawled along the roof of the bus and put his hand down the front of the windscreen - giving the driver a near heart attack. So the story goes...

In his memories, Eddie Unwin mentioned Jimmy Todd, he of the brute strength. Jimmy was a driver at Berwick in my time. He used to drive in from Norham in a little 3-wheeler Morgan. It leant heavily to one side as he drove up the Bus Station. Morgan broke down at Middle Ord one day. A passing motorist stopped to see Jimmy turning the starting handle fiercely with Morgan on the other end. 'Jimmy, be careful - that thing'll fly off the handle and kill somebody!'.

Another Todd is JAMES TODD, of the SMT, and nothing to do with the Jimmy Todd above. The only similarity lies in the name. James Todd came from Melrose. He started as a conductor with Brook & Amos in 1923. He was their first, even before Jimmy Elder. He went driving with them becoming a Ticket Inspector in 1949. In 1952 he became District Superintendent at Kelso then, in 1953, replaced Jimmy Elder at Berwick. He was a quiet man, a bit dour in manner, but with a drole sense of humour. He died before I started research for this book so I missed a man with a wealth of memories.

Just before the demise of United in 1986, Berwick staff decorated this Bristol LH for a local carnival. Showing off the 'Mississippi Steam Boat' are Helena Richardson and Liz Jones.

At United's Wooler depot was JOHN HODGE. He went there as an 18 year old conductor in April 1939. 'I had worked on the farm but in 1938 I joined the Supplementary Reserve so I was in the Army for 6 months. After that I started as a conductor. For training, we had to go to Alnwick where Jimmy Slight was the Instructor. He, and Tommy Hindmarsh, were the Inspectors there, both good lads', he said. 'At first I worked at Wooler. I got a bit more than £1.00 a week. The drivers had to do repairs on the road. They all carried their little bags, their tool kits.

'Wooler had a full staff, but Alnwick was short.' Confirming what Eddie Unwin had told me earlier, John said, 'I was told to go to Alnwick and had to lodge there. I had a terrible job to get an employee's pass to get to and from home Eventually they gave me a 12-journey ticket which was clipped every time I travelled. You had to pay lodgings out of your pay. Alnwick was short of staff, but Seahouses was worse, so I was told to go to Seahouses. I had to get lodgings there, and to get home to Wooler, I had to go via Alnwick. The buses along the coast were busy all the time. We carried a lot of parcels

as well, a lot of newspapers, milk and boxes of kippers from Craster. Seahouses crews had to clean their own buses; the driver cleaned the outside and the conductor cleaned the inside. The first bus went out on service 29 at 6.0am. We had to come in at 5.0am to clean that bus after the previous day's passengers. Inspector Heseltine was the Wooler Inspector then. He used to come from Wooler on his motor bike to check that we were in. He would be waiting at the door at 5.0am for us.

'As I had been in the Supplementary Reserve, I got my calling up papers two days before the War started, so I was called up from Seahouses.'

John came back from the Army in 1946 and returned to Wooler as a conductor. 'I did conducting for a year, then went into the driving school, staying at Wooler until I retired in 1985. We worked service 15 to Newcastle and Edinburgh, 21 and 70 to Alnwick, 64 to Berwick and 71 to Yetholm. We had a lot of AECs, the ARO type. Arthur MacLean was the Depot Foreman; the buses were kept in excellent order and I think Wooler had the best maintained buses in Northumberland.'

A more recent 'temporary' conductor at Wooler was ALAN BROWN. He got a job there for six weeks in 1955. Those six weeks went on for three years when he became a driver. They went on long enough for Alan to retire in 1997 after 42 years at Wooler. 'I was only ever booked once by an Inspector, it was for carrying a cat without a ticket. In those days all livestock had to have a ticket, but this day I had a woman on my bus with a box. I didn't know at the time there was a cat in it! I went on to become Driver in Charge at Wooler in 1980. I enjoyed my years in the industry - and I did achieve something!'

Alan still has a well-thumbed notebook from his time in the conductors' training school. One of the vast number of instructions it contains relates to passengers unable to pay their fare. 'Any person unable to pay an authorised fare in excess of 3d on stage carriage vehicles or 1/- on express services must be refused travel unless the person is known to the driver or conductor or can be vouched for by another fare-paying passenger known to the crew'. But just to make sure, the conductor had to issue a ticket and put in a report with the name and address. He would be charged for that ticket if it wasn't paid!

The conductors' school at Newcastle was run

Wooler drivers - Safe Driving Awards 1964. Front row: Canon Rawson, Mr J.H.Farrar, Mr J.H.Pratt, Arthur McLean, Depot Foreman. Back row: J.Hodge, R.Stewart, T.Purvis, J.Russell, A.Brown, W.Bertram, J.Stevenson, S.Batey, W.Knox, J.Riddell, J.Smith.

by Inspector Jimmy Southall. He was another who started as a conductor about his 18th birthday and spent his life with United, first at Berwick, then as Road Inspector, Training Inspector, and Chief Inspector at Middlesbrough. His family had the Red Lion at Allanton for many years. What I have written above only touches on some of the people I knew and worked with. From United, from SMT, from Berwick, Alnwick, Wooler and Kelso they came, with a degree of loyalty and public service unequalled.

For myself, I left Berwick in September 1953 to work in United's District Office in Gallowgate, Newcastle. It lacked the humour we had at Berwick but it had its odd moments. We had to clock in and out. They had a time clock

built for contortionists. It worked by a handle on the right side. Being right-handed you had to reach across with the left hand, pull the handle towards you and hold it down while you signed your name in the aperture. OK - if you were left-handed.

The Office Manager, Jimmy Hindmarsh, was a

More Wooler staff in the 1960s. Driver Alec Campbell, conductresses Peggy Tait, Sheila Purvis, Nancy Robson, Sheila Cullingworth, Jean Straughan.

Service 69. Berwick—Philadelphia.
(For Scremerston Beach).

THURSDAYS AND SUNDAYS ONLY.

FARES. Sgle. s. d.	Rtn. s. d.				pm	pm	
0 1½	—	BERWICK (Marygate)	dept.	2 15	6 0	..	
0 2	—	Tweedmouth (Railway Arches) .	,,	2 18	6 3	..	
0 3	0 5	Springhill	,,	2 23	6 8	..	
0 5	0 9	Scremerston (Co-op.)	,,	2 27	6 12	..	
		PHILADELPHIA (Cafe) ...	arr.	2 35	6 20	..	

Sgle. s. d.	Rtn. s. d.				pm	pm	pm
0 2	0 3	PHILADELPHIA (Cafe) ..	dept.	4 30	6 30	8 0	
0 3	0 5	Scremerston (Co-op.) ..	,,	4 38	6 38	8 8	
0 4	0 7	Springhill	,,	4 42	6 42	8 12	
0 5	0 9	Tweedmouth (Railway Arches) ..	,,	4 47	6 47	8 17	
		BERWICK (Marygate) ..	arr.	4 50	6 50	8 20	

United timetable for Summer 1934. This is an ex-Thompson service.

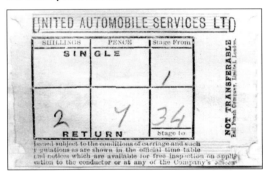

short, slim man. The office corridors had partial opaque glass, the panels of which were just too high for him to see over. In case he missed anything, he used to go along the corridor rising on tiptoes to see into the offices. He got known as 'the ballet dancer.' He placed great store on the time clock and the quality of his inspection of the rolls was legendary. However he did not see the vulnerability of the payroll being carried by hand through Berwick.

Looking back, years later when I had risen to the dizzy heights of management, I had one thing to thank Gallowgate, and Jimmy Hindmarsh, for - how not to manage people. Gordon Wilson, at Berwick, had taught the other useful lesson - what to do in the real world of buses. Both lessons would stay with me.